Impact, ~~Results, Outcomes~~

"Keep writing, your work is a pleasure to read, thank you."

– Sarah Camacho

"Thank you a million for having changed my life already. I feel indebted to you. I hope your children know your true value and what you can bring to them. They are lucky to have you."

– Marc Hammoud

"I have to say I'm loving your posts. They are engaging, insightful and fun! Thanks for taking the time to write them up. I now just read yours and Seth Godin's."

– Conor McCarthy

"I attended my first event last night and was very impressed with how it was run and with your presentation. I came away feeling very motivated and focused to achieve what I set out to in the next month."

– Natalie Game

"Loving your daily doses of inspiration. Thanks Scott."

– Angela Ahmed

"I am doing exactly as you suggested. Started by waking up early to make space in my day for my goals and dreams. I am going for a walk every morning and started learning Russian and also started contacting people on LinkedIn; I am loving all these adjustments in my life."

– Diana Franco

CREATE YOUR FATE

BEFORE IT'S TOO LATE

"The starting point of all achievement is desire."

–Napoleon Hill

ACHIEVE ANYTHING

The 7 Simple Steps
to Shift from Uncomfortable
to Unstoppable

Scott Gregory

Grosvenor House
Publishing Limited

This book is published by
Grosvenor House Publishing Ltd
Link House
140 The Broadway, Tolworth, Surrey, KT6 7HT.
www.grosvenorhousepublishing.co.uk

A CIP record for this book
is available from the British Library

ISBN 978-1-83975-825-6

This book is dedicated to my three wonderful children,
Axel, Ryker and Skyler.

May you achieve anything you wish to pursue and
find great joy in all that you achieve.

ACKNOWLEDGMENTS

For starting me out in life and setting my on a wonderful path, I would like to thank my Mom, Barbara Gregory and my Dad, Alan Gregory. Your guidance, support and encouragement has helped me achieve many great things.

My wonderful wife Roxane was amazing in her support, coaxing encouragement and patience, as well as her detailed feedback, which helped improve the readability of the manuscript. For all of that, the great cover design and much, much more, I love and thank you so very dearly.

My three children have given me inspiration and encouragement and have been patient while prompting me to complete this book. Thanks kids!

A big thank you to my editor Doug Williams for his insights, careful review, encouragement and patience. Also, big thanks to the GHP team, especially Becky Banning and Dean Zaltsman for getting this over the line.

I would also like to thank people who helped in the early days and throughout with encouragement, inspiration, ideas and motivation. Their continual support and cheering helped ensure I got this book over the finish line. So a huge thank you to Sharon O'Pray, Julie Cudlipp and Alex Cooper. Sharon and Julie's feedback after reading the manuscript was excellent and encouraging. Alex's energy, optimism, insights and ideas helped keep things moving forward.

In addition, other invaluable key supporters who asked me about the book and encouraged me to complete it were Paul Brady, Juliet Brady, Christine Adams, Colin Adams, Fiona Dickinson, Mark Dickinson, Mike Smith, Tom Bird, Helena Bird, Diana Franco, Mark Wrigglesworth, Kevette Minor Kane, Egle Thomas, Wendy Pease, Andrew Francis and Eric Moeller. This includes Clare Brazeau and Don Brazeau for your years of support and for raising such a great daughter.

A big thank you to authors Mike Cordy, Eric Duneau and Christian Rodwell for their time and insight into the writing world, publishing, agents, resources, contacts and the challenges and benefits of writing.

There were also many people who supported me online and on social media by liking, commenting on, or sharing my blog posts or who provided feedback or encouraging words. Unknown maybe to you, these positive actions were incredibly helpful in letting me understand that my thoughts and ideas were having a beneficial impact. Some of you I've already mentioned above so these thank you's are to Celine Smith, Angela Ahmed, Sarah Camacho, Conor McCarthy, and Sean Croxton of The Quote of the Day Show.

Thanks to Chris Kasgorgis and Alex for building scottsbook. com and scottsthinking.com.

Thank you to those people who have inspired or guided the creation of this book: Jim Rohn, MJ DeMarco, Robert Kiyosaki, Raymond Aaron and Chandler Bolt.

There were many other people who have commented, wished me luck or encouraged me in one way or another. It has been invaluable and greatly appreciated. Thank you!!!!

PREFACE

There are many reasons to write a book like this one.

My original thought was to create a book of useful advice for my children to read as they grew up and to reference as adults. I wanted them to know how I thought and how they could achieve anything they set their minds to. If only they could have the formula early on in life, perhaps they would be able to achieve even more than they could dream of.

Then, as I began to write the book, I realized it was a great way to organize my own thoughts on the topic of achievement. I realized I was working through my own 'aha' moments and it felt great to get a real grip on how, and why, it all comes together.

Finally, as I began to write more and get into the detail and core philosophy, I realized that there were many people looking for the same sort of directional advice. The more I spoke to people, the more I could see that this seven-step approach would be ideal for people to use. Sometimes it would be simple things that people had forgotten. Other times, it would be ideas not yet heard. Whichever it was, most people were grateful to hear the advice, tips, or tricks that they could use immediately to benefit their lives.

Becoming uncomfortable is a slow process due to a lack of daily investment in yourself. This book will help you as you shift from uncomfortable to unstoppable and achieve the very things you thought were out of your reach.

I hope that the work that I have put into this book will serve you now and for many years to come. Your effort in reading and following the recommendations in this book will pay off handsomely. You will grow in confidence and achieve further success in many areas of your life. Some will be long-forgotten dreams and others will be unexpected new opportunities.

I wish you the very best in your desire to shift from where you are to where you want to be.

Make your actions deliver your dreams.

CONTENTS

ACKNOWLEDGMENTS   **ix**

PREFACE   **xi**

INTRODUCTION   **xvii**

STEP 1 - THINK   **1**

    1.   Start at the finish   2

        I.   Where do I want to be?   3

        II.   Start with the fun bit of creating
            a destiny worth living   4

        III. Life: As simple as planning
            a holiday   6

    2.   Mindset   8

        I.   Fixed and growth   18

        II.   Programming challenges and fun   20

        III. Something for the pain   22

        IV. The power of the mind   26

STEP 2 - OVERCOME 33

3.   Current beliefs, ideas, thoughts 35
- I.   Fear - The great barrier belief 37
- II.   Money challenges 41
- III.   Challenge your Why 43
- IV.   Map out how to remove, detour around or change beliefs 47

4.   Regret: Woulda, coulda, shoulda 51
- I.   Let bygones be 52
- II.   Five minutes to freak out 53

5.   Rewrite your programming 55
- I.   Appreciation and gratitude 55
- II.   Visualize 58

STEP 3 - WRITE 69

6.   The Imagination Game 70
- I.   Imagination: Use it or lose it 70
- II.   Assessing and sorting 71
- III.   Break out - Your get out of jail free card 72

7.   Decide what you want (and write it down) 75
- I.   Select the best Imagination Game ideas; Sifting while shifting 83
- II.   Understand your Why for going after the goal 84
- III.   Go bigger 87

8.   Set Goals 91
- I.   What is a goal? 91
- II.   Why have goals? 93
- III.   You already have goals 94
- IV.   Be SMART with your goals 96

CONTENTS

STEP 4 - PLAN   103

9.   Understand clearly where you are   106
     I.   Note the precise distance and
           direction you need to travel   112

10. Prioritize and structure goals   114
     I.   Timeframes for each goal - day,
           week, month, year   115
     II.   MTO (Minimum, Target, Outrageous)   118
     III. The 7-Day Success Cycle   119

11. Map key activities and milestones   123

STEP 5 - ACT   131

12. Decision, Commitment, Resolve: Until!   132

13. Act as if   137

14. Mini or massive action   140
     I.   The knowing-doing gap   140
     II.   Procrastination   142
     III. Prepare to struggle before success   145

STEP 6 - REVIEW   151

15. Achieve & Believe   153
     I.   Achieve smaller goals   153
     II.   Getting movement   155
     III   Growing confidence   156

16. Course-correct   159
     I.   Airplanes: From manual to autopilot   159
     II.   Pivot point (if getting off course
           gets out of hand)   164

17. Repeat   167
    I.   Written log   167
    II. Gamify your progress   168
    III. Review and smile   170

STEP 7 - CELEBRATE   **175**

18. Every little and big goal achievement   177
    I.   Little and often   177
    II. Keep a list of achievements (words,
         pictures, mementos)   179
    III. Plan some nice things   180

19. Grow belief and confidence through
    achievement   182
    I.   Pride   182
    II. Determination   182

20. Gratitude   184

FINAL WORD   **187**

**VISIT MY WEBSITE AND SOCIAL
MEDIA PAGES**   **188**

RESOURCES   **189**

IF YOU FOUND THIS BOOK USEFUL   **190**

POSTSCRIPT: NOW, ACHIEVE ANYTHING!   **191**

INTRODUCTION

What's making you uncomfortable right now? What isn't exactly how you want it to be in your life? Your boss? Your career? Your holidays? Health and fitness? Your relationships? Your finances? Or is it just life itself, with how fast it zooms by every day without you having achieved all those things you had dreamed of doing, being, or having?

Consider these areas of your life on a scale of 1 to 10. If you think there is a little room for improvement in some of these areas, I know this book will help.

Are you where you wanted to be?

I believe most people would get a little uncomfortable if they had to confront the brutal facts of their life and where they are now. This would be even more likely if they considered their reality in relation to where they may have casually thought, dreamed, or convinced themselves of where they would be, or should be, by now. With time ticking away and life getting in the way, it sometimes seems impossible to achieve even the most basic goals we let pass through our heads. Never mind the more exciting, audacious, or lucrative goals we at one time dreamed about for ourselves.

It doesn't have to be that way

Any feeling of being uncomfortable due to a lack of time, lost or wasted opportunities, helplessness, general discomfort, or regret no longer need to be your feelings. You have the good fortune of having found this book. You, dear reader, are standing on a precipice. In the next few seconds or minutes, one of those key life moments will arrive where you will make a life-altering decision. You can decide to grab this book, pull the wisdom out of it, make it your life map, and start experiencing level 10 happiness in one, some, or all of the areas of your life above. Or you can quietly return it to the shelf, walk away, and wonder, for the rest of your life, whether you really did have it in you to be better, raise your standards, find excellence and become an unstoppable force.

Transform yourself today

I have seen rapid transformations in the people who decide to invest the effort, follow the directions, and make the changes required. There is a simple formula to achieve anything in life. I will walk you through it. The road you are about to travel may not always be easy. You will need to make adjustments to your environment, while building discipline and gratitude into your life. However, I am certain that, if you commit to the process, and follow it diligently, you will thrive and live the most exciting life you can imagine for yourself.

This could very well be the last self-help or personal development book you'll ever need.

Your exciting new life

Are you the type of person who wants to get up and do exciting things, leave their job, travel around the world, shed a few pounds, ask someone out, quit something, start something, live overseas, buy a villa in paradise, go diving with sharks, or be financially free? If you said "yes," then this is the book for you. I've done these things and much more and I want to show you the 7 simple steps that I used, so you can do some of these things, or all of them, and many others.

In addition to experience of my own, I've learned from others as they achieved their goals. I've read countless books and articles on the topic, watched and listened to 1,000s of hours of video and audio, made observations and also simply reflected. This book isn't a theoretical treatise, philosophical paper, doctoral diatribe, or research record. This is "been there, done that," real life adventure stuff. I'm a regular guy who wants to help other regular people do exciting or extraordinary things. This book will even help those of you who simply want to achieve success with more standard life activities such as finding a better job, becoming financially free, or preparing for retirement. Or it could be as simple as being keen to up your game in areas like fitness, health, and family life.

You may find the secret to success in here. Your secret. Undoubtedly though, in this book you will find some useful tips about the process of shifting from uncomfortable to unstoppable.

If you're not crazy delighted with where you are in life right now, then this book is for you.

That's if you are the kind of person who wants more out of life but haven't yet been able to master the game, or if you want just a little bit more but don't know what you're looking for, or if maybe you want a whole lot more, but you can't seem to make the headway. *Then this is your book.*

You can have this dream too

Were you told as a kid that you could be anything, do anything, achieve anything? Or maybe you weren't told that as a child, but you tell your children or friends these very words to encourage them. With that in mind, are you feeling you are living up to that promise right now? Did you almost believe it was true but weren't sure if you should? Did you totally believe it and tell everyone in sight? Did you walk around thinking it was true, but just not yet for you and all of your dreams and aspirations? Maybe you even thought it was complete nonsense, hyperbole, and impossible, but then you wonder because you read about people doing amazing, wonderful, joyous, delicious things every day, either in the newspaper, in magazines, or on the web.

Well, you see, it is true. You can Achieve Anything. And soon you'll see this is true for you too.

Why this book now?

Why do you need to read this book now? It contains the process for all achievement. It contains the basics. Yes, the basics. To achieve anything in life, you will need to follow a process. Some processes are better than others. Some will save you time. Some will save you money. Some will save your sanity. The process of achievement that I have outlined in this book will save you all three: time, money, and sanity. If the process is followed, acted upon, and developed as a consistent habit in your life, you will, in a short space of time, be able to achieve anything your heart desires and your mind can conceive.

Remember that airplanes, color televisions, the internet, walking on the moon and mobile phones were all inconceivable impossibilities throughout most of recorded history — some even as recently as 50 years ago. However, someone conceived the idea in their mind and brought it into existence through action, study, feedback, and focus.

You have all the tools required to make simple or amazing things happen. Read this book and start today. Build a better life for yourself and for others around you. Maybe you will even have a profound impact on the world! Let's do this together and you'll find that you can indeed achieve anything. Let's go!

How to read this book:

Immerse yourself! Get a pen, highlighter, and pencil and mark up this book with your thoughts and preferred references. Highlight key passages you want to remember or revisit. Make notes in the margins to remind yourself of key messages or thoughts. Make this book your workbook for life.

Then use it or lose it as the saying goes. An egg on the shelf looks nice and tidy, but if you are hungry, it's much more useful to break the egg into a frying pan and make it how you like it. Add ketchup, bacon, or toast to truly make it yours. Do the same with this book. Make it yours. You can then share it or keep it to yourself. If you don't want others to see what you've highlighted or written in the margins, then suggest they buy their own copy or buy it for them as a gift.

Read and refer to this book at least one time every year. More often if you are serious about achievement. Review your notes, and the passages you've underlined, on a daily, weekly and at least a monthly basis. Review, re-read, and remember your key observations until you have ingrained the whole thing into your mind, habits and soul. Even then, keep re-reading this book once a year (at least) until the final year of your life.

It will be your most valuable resource. Your trusted companion.

It will change your life in ways you can't even imagine at the moment.

So as Matt Theriault often says, "move at the speed of instruction and travel as far as you can see... and when you get there you can see further."

Now, let's begin with the end in mind as Stephen Covey would suggest. Grab your pen, pencil and highlighter and let's get started.

STEP 1 - **THINK**

Thinking is one of the hardest things you can do. It is not to be confused with reading, listening, or watching. Nor is it defined by immediately agreeing or disagreeing. It is not your emotional reaction. Thinking is "the process of considering or reasoning about something," according to Oxford Languages.

You know when you've been thinking. It hurts a little. You've stepped, figuratively, into other people's shoes and run your hypotheses through their brain. You've considered their point of view. You've played chess with the future to assess the optimal outcome. This is not easy.

"What is the hardest task in the world? To think."

- Ralph Waldo Emerson

Thinking can even make you uncomfortable. You may realize some things you hadn't considered before. These thoughts may challenge you, but I know you can handle it.

To achieve anything in life, you need to be ready. By reading this far, I am sure you are ready. By this I mean ready to do some thinking, some planning and taking new actions with new and exciting results!

Transformation begins in the mind. And now that you've started on this journey, let's take a look at how amazing your life will be at the end of it.

Chapter 1. Start at the finish

There you are. You're relaxed and resting on a swaying hammock, in the shade of a tall, calming palm tree. You have a cool beverage in one hand and a fascinating book on the table beside you. You're looking out over the glistening, turquoise blue sea. The warm air is moving gently around you in a light and pleasant breeze. You gaze out at the distant horizon and reflect back on your amazing journey to this lovely, idyllic beach. The soft breaking of the rolling waves brings you back into the present.

That might be the destination you have in mind. Or your future may look a little different. Perhaps you are skiing, climbing a mountain, or speaking at a convocation. Whatever you would like your life to look like in the future, picture it.

"Begin with the end in mind"

- Stephen Covey

Dream, consider, and visualize all the pieces of your exceptional life in the not-too-distant future. It is now there waiting for you. You simply need to build the bridge from here to there and connect these two realities: your present one and your preferred future one. Now that is what we are going to do together.

"If you have built castles in the air, your work need not be lost; that is where they should be. Now put the foundations under them."

- Henry David Thoreau

Now maybe there are too many dreams swirling around in your head. So many ideas for you to pursue or choose from.

This may mean you have not moved toward any of them sufficiently. This could be the reason for the slightly uncomfortable feelings you have been experiencing.

Remember this. Even if you don't know where you are going, you are going somewhere. So as much as you might be uncertain, or uncomfortable, your first step is to understand your end game.

The first thing you need to realize is that, in this game of life, you won't get out alive. At the end of the game, there is no restart. As far as most people can tell, your mind will go quiet and your body will stop moving. There may be something else after all of this. That is something for you to consider with your beliefs. But as far as your friends and family are concerned, they won't be inviting you over for lunch again anytime soon.

Now you are aware that you need to see the finish before you begin. With that in mind, let's start to find the right finish for you.

I. Where do I want to be?

"If you don't know where you are going, any road will get you there."

- Lewis Carroll

If you are honest with yourself, you may already know where you want to be. And if you don't know, start with thinking about your youth. Thinking about your younger days can often provide a window into what you value most. Remember, thinking is "the process of considering or reasoning about something." This is very important work. So stick with it for a minute or two.

What did you want to do in life that got you excited? How did you want to live?

Think back to when you were 8 years old or 10, 12, 16, or even 18. This decade can be a very illuminating time. Everything was pretty new and exciting. What grabbed your attention? Some people liked writing, while others were mad about sports. A few people knew they would go to university or were certain they would become a doctor or live in a different place.

Give yourself a few minutes to simply reflect on what you want today and what you wanted in your youth. Assess these ideas and write down a few of your favorite headline ideas at the top of the page or on a separate note pad. For additional ideas and a worksheet that will help you dive deeper with this exercise, go to www.scottsbook.com/achieveanything/ resources and click on the sheet called "What do I want?"

All of your ideas or thoughts are valid. They are a part of you. Let them come out. You may find some answers in there that you had forgotten about.

II. Start with the fun bit of creating a destiny worth living

You may have been thinking about your career, home, wealth, relationships, health, or hobbies. You might have noticed that the pictures you were starting to form in your mind were already assuming some ideas that you hadn't made explicit yet.

You may have assumed you were healthy and had a certain physique. In creating your ideal home, you may have inadvertently added in a partner, children, pets, and wealth indicators. You may have an idea about your desired size of home, location, neighborhood, friends, etc.

If you have your creative juices flowing, this would be a great time to put down the book and write out a few notes in a journal, on a pad of paper, or on a napkin. Or you can put your notes into a device. Borrow some paper from someone if you need to. You could even borrow a device and email it to yourself — just be sure to give it back! It's brilliant to get some of these ideas down as they occur to you, because sometimes they disappear and then are harder than you would think to find again.

Being open and curious sure can help. Have fun with this part. Get creative and dream a little. Dream a lot. This is just for you. You can keep these thoughts to yourself at the moment. I just hope they excite you and get you more interested in your incredible and fascinating future.

The following is a list of questions which should help you with this exercise:

- What does your energy draw you toward? (Books, people, sport, relationships?)
- Who is your favorite actor and actress? What characteristics do they have that you like?
- Where would you like to live? (Beach, mountains, city, town, condo, house?)
- How much money would you need to cover your monthly expenses in your new life?
- What type of jobs do you like to do? (Physical, technical, office, outdoors, entertainer?)
- Whose physique would inspire you to emulate them?
- If you can imagine any future for yourself, why not make it exciting and fascinating?

III. Life: As simple as planning a holiday

My favorite way to describe how to start at the finish is by using a travel analogy. Now many of you will have been on some kind of holiday, family visit, trip, or even a local outing at some point in your life. And planning to achieve anything is very similar to the planning you naturally do when you are going on a holiday.

The first thing you do is decide you want to go somewhere. Then you need to decide where it is you want to go. This might be just to your sofa, to a local park for the afternoon, Gramma's for the weekend, or a three-week, all-inclusive golf/spa retreat in the Caribbean.

Whichever it is, the process is the same. Decide where you want to go and what it will be like when you get there.

Then you can agree on the dates, ensure it's in your budget, and start planning the details. You will need to be precise in noting how and when you are going and returning. Also, you will want to be clear about what you will do while you are there. The reason being is that you may need to book accommodations, restaurants, activities, and any required modes of travel.

Achieving anything in life is all a rather simple procedure. It is a process you almost certainly use for many aspects of your life. You do this process to go to school or work. You do this when you want to watch a movie or tv in the evening. You also do this nearly every time you would like something to eat. You think of, or "see," what you would like and set off on a path of simple steps to bring it into your present reality.

So why does this seem so difficult to do sometimes?

The answer to that million-dollar question is found in the very next chapter.

KEY POINTS
CHAPTER 1 – START AT THE FINISH

- Dream about your exceptional future life.

- You are going somewhere. You better find out where!

- Find the right finish for you.

- Create a destiny worth living.

- Plan your life like you would a holiday.

- Take intentional and focused action to bring your dream and plan into reality.

Chapter 2. Mindset

Mindset! This may be the most important part of this book. This is the most important part of any journey. This is the most important part of any personal development and any personal transformation. If you can master your mind, you can master anything. Good thing you've read this far!

> *"We become what we think about most of the time, and that's the strangest secret."*
>
> **- Earl Nightingale**

Shifting - from you to you+:

You will need to give up the story of your life (the one you have) to create the story of your life (the one you want).

This can be quite scary for people as they are potentially walking away from their known entity and might become "someone else" — an uncomfortable proposition to many people! But in reality, you only ever become a different version of yourself. A better version or a worse version, but you always remain you. Some people say, "Oh, that just isn't me," and they are right — given the story they have of who they are and the picture they have in their mind. And given the story and the picture, we then (psychologically speaking) must act congruently within those parameters.

So, to begin the process of shifting, you can start by reimagining your story and the picture you have in your mind of yourself and your situation. The following is a visualization technique that might help you see past the self-confining walls you may have inadvertently created for yourself.

Think of a mime getting out of a small box. First, they push on one side and reimagine it being larger with more space. Then they push on the other side and give it more space there too. Then they can push on the top and stand up straight in it, spreading themselves out and stretching up tall and comfortable. Reimagine you have more space to be you. Push on the boundary walls that are keeping you a prisoner. Move those barriers a little farther away. You may find this liberating or a little uncomfortable. Then relax until you get comfortable again. As with exposure therapy, you think about something that makes you uncomfortable and sit with that slight discomfort until you see it as a normal situation or until the discomfort goes away. Deep breathing will help as you work through this exercise.

We will cover visualization, exposure therapy, and several other tactics in greater depth as we move through the book. If you are interested in more free resources on these topics, go to www.scottsbook.com/achieveanything.

"I must be willing to give up what I am in order to become what I will be."

- Albert Einstein

Is this the end me? The real me? The final and forever me? Or is this just a temporary me? A fleeting me for this moment? Is this just one step of many me's or of a million me's? Do I shed mental me's like a snake sheds its skin? As an adult, it is harder to see that "me" is constantly changing. Sometimes the change is a gigantic, noticeable one for all to see, such as a new partner, hairstyle, or profession. But usually it is a very small, nuanced, directional change that only very perceptive people will notice at first, and others will notice as that element becomes more observable.

However, as a child we see, feel, and know we are changing significantly, all the time. We get used to different physical and mental changes in the first 20 years of our life. Everyone else can see the big changes here too. We go through so many versions of "me." We start with wet-diapers-me and then baby-talk-me, stumble-and-walking-me, year-3-me, 10-year-old-me, sporty-me, teenage-me, etc.

Life begins with the noticeable changes being more physical and then the shift is more dramatic in the mind from 2 to 20 years old. Although we can see the physical changes and hear the corresponding, "My how you've grown" comments, the mind is developing incredibly quickly.

We don't usually stop to think about who we are and whether we like what we are becoming. Or at least not until it gets close to being too late. There will be moments we would like to freeze in time and others that we can't wait to end and hope never to revisit.

However, no matter how many versions of yourself you go through, you are still you. You could be conservative you or liberal you. You can be friendly or distant. But the changes come from the thoughts you develop in your mind. It then directs your brain to do what is necessary to make the changes you are requesting.

You can now see how nothing is off limits and described as "not me." It may simply be not you anymore or not yet. Still, it could be a future version of you, if you allow yourself to try it on. Like shirts when you go shopping, you can try them on and then remove them. The ones you like, you purchase and take into the future with you. Sometimes you have to try it on and see how it feels, rather than just see it on the hanger. This is exposure therapy again and it's quite an important concept to get comfortable with. It allows you the space to try out characteristics that you want without reducing your options down to only a few at the outset.

Some questions you can use to help you consider alternative-you scenarios are:

A. How would it feel to give a speech, sing a song, or perform in front of a crowd?
B. How do I feel when I am involved in a fast-paced environment? (Chef or server in a busy restaurant, ambulance worker, financial trader)
C. Can you see yourself as a healthy, fit individual standing tall and confident?
D. Would I be comfortable sharing my life with someone else and the occasional compromises that may require?

Clarity of thought and precision of action:

You need to be absolutely clear in your thoughts. You need to be completely aware of what your mind is thinking, why it is thinking that, and how that is affecting your results.

Your mind is very much like a computer. It takes input, processes it, and delivers an output. The mind is essentially the same for everyone. In your early years, you take in significant amounts of information: visual, tactile, and auditory. Your mind then processes this information, and makes some assumptions, which creates your beliefs and values. From these values and beliefs, you will form your philosophy of life and your habits. These habits become your daily thoughts and then actions. Your daily actions determine your daily outcomes.

The process is quite simple.

It is also the same for everybody else. Just like turning on a light, you will find that performing a certain process will almost always deliver the same result. If you were to just sit on your chair and look at the light switch, hoping for the light to turn on, what result do you think you would get? Unless you were Yoda, or had some other Jedi-like powers, the light would not turn on, and over time you would get frustrated. Your frustration would stem from a desired or expected outcome not being met by your reality, despite how much you wanted it to happen. This Expectation versus Reality Gap (ER Gap) is explored later on in the chapter.

In what areas is this "hoping but not happening" becoming obvious in your life at the moment? Write a brief list right now.

Here are a few prompts to help you with your list:

- Would you like to lose some weight and feel fitter and more confident?
- Have you tried to quit or cut back on smoking, drinking, or worrying?
- Would you like to be earning more money?
- Would you like more time in your life for you?
- Is slight anxiety replacing smiles and happiness in your life?

It's great to get your list out of your mind. It helps you realize that it is not an endless list. There may be a few items or quite a few. Regardless, it's a manageable group of items which many people share as common desires. So you are not alone in this. The great news is that you can improve in all of these areas. You simply need to follow the processes as outlined in this book and you will start seeing improvements very quickly.

Of course you could sort out the situation, and get the result you desire, by simply finding a way to turn on the light. This could be as simple as standing up, walking across the room, and turning the light switch to «on" yourself. Or you could get creative, and request that somebody turn the light on for you. Alternatively, find a stick that could reach the light switch from where you were sitting and turn it on that way. Otherwise, you could find a ball near you that you could throw at the light switch to have it turn on. The simple point is that you need to do more than have positive thought, though positive thinking is a good place to start as it warms you up to believe you may be able to achieve it. In addition, you need to have some sort of action. In this case, it would be standing up and walking, using your voice to request help, making some sort of gesture to somebody else, or using a stick or a ball. You see, until you develop the mental skills of a Jedi, you are required to physically take "out of mind" action to get results on planet Earth.

If you are taking action and not getting the results you want, that is a different challenge to address. So, carrying on with our light switch example, if your action was to ask someone to open the door, even though you wanted the light switched on, you would not get the result that you wanted. Or, if you picked up a stick and pushed a book across the floor with it, you would not get the result of having the light turn on either. In these instances, you need to become aware of what your mind is thinking. You need to be crystal clear on what outcome you are seeking. Armed with that clarity of thought, you can then seek out the best process you can use to affect that outcome.

Simple? Yes. Easy? Depends.

As with so many things in life, it is simple, but not always easy, to reflect on and understand what your mind is thinking. You need to dissect the thoughts and desires you have in your mind, either in pictorial or word format, and be absolutely clear on what you want.

You can figure this out on your own at first. Or you can do an online search and see what other successful people are doing. It is essential to get going at the start though. Once you are moving forward, then you can consider how to find the best, most effective, most efficient ways of doing a process to get the result you want. But first do some mental work and see what you come up with.

Remember this too. Sometimes it is easier to eliminate things at the beginning. So if there are things you know you absolutely don't want, put them on a list too. Occasionally looking at the list of things you do not want will help you understand what you do want. What you want can be as simple as being the opposite of those things you don't want.

Here is a list of things you probably don't want. You can use it to help get you started:

- I don't want to be overweight.
- I don't want a divorce or break-up.
- I don't want to die of a heart attack.
- I would not like to lose my job.
- I do not want to be unhappy.
- I don't want to go broke or be poor.
- I don't want to be lonely.

Don't spend too much time on all the don't want items. But do use it to help you think about things you do want. They are often the opposite of anything you don't want. Those are then the things you want to focus on and repeat.

The trouble with dwelling on things you don't want is that they become your focus. Of course you won't be hoping for them to come into your life. However, you may spend time worrying about them coming into your life. You may even spend time trying to avoid them and keeping them out of your life. Spend little to no energy on thoughts of what you don't want.

Remember, worrying is like praying for bad stuff to happen. Pray for the good things.

Not getting the results you want:

If you are not getting the results that you want, then you need to assess why that is happening. Again, this is simple to say but still somewhat challenging to do, especially on your own.

I heard a great turn of phrase the other day. It was: "You can't see the full picture if you are in the picture." I thought that was a great graphic way of describing the idea. It's good to have a coach, mentor, or someone who will at least provide feedback to you so that you can be made aware of the blind spots you have and the things you can't see from where you are (in the picture). You either need a tool, like a mirror, to see how you look, or you need someone outside of the picture to make you aware. It is the same with anything in life. If honest and open feedback is what you want, then having someone outside the picture (not you, your family or friends) can be a very useful way to achieve that.

"People would do better, if they knew better."

–Jim Rohn

So trying to assess what you need to do differently can be challenging. Often we don't like to address the truth or reality of our situation or our life. Most people avoid this or make up stories that they sell to themselves. These stories suit their mindset and situation, so they don't hurt their own egos. So when it comes to being objective about our own personal situation, we often misjudge, misinterpret, avoid, underestimate, and overestimate the things we do. This means we are likely to have incorrect or misleading feedback to work from. Furthermore, if you start with inaccurate feedback about the current situation, you are likely to provide the wrong or ineffective corrections to the situation. This has the potential to make matters worse rather than better. At least it is unlikely that you will make any material improvement. It's all about where you start in mind, philosophy, or body.

To give you an example of this, I was thinking about how much time people spend on something and how much less time it would take if they had a seasoned professional in that sphere help them. I remember talking about writing a book. I remember telling a few people about doing this for several years. Then I started realizing that, although I was talking about writing a book, I wasn't actually writing a book. In fact, in the early days, I wasn't writing anything at all. I had a few plans in my head: I had ideas, I had titles, chapter ideas, website ideas, and new marketing ideas. This wasn't getting me to the result I wanted, which was an actual book that I had written.

Then I started to write down my conceptual ideas, chapter titles, and marketing ideas. Next, I started to learn more about how many words I would need to write in total to create a saleable, non-fiction book. I took a course on writing a book. I even followed the process of the course for about eight weeks. Then I stopped following the course for various reasons and didn't get restarted. After all of that, I started reading books about writing books and following the points made in these books. I would also listen to podcasts and read online to further help me understand what I needed to do to complete the writing of my book, get it published, marketed, and make significant sales.

To achieve this, my to-do list would include completing the first draft, having it edited, getting a cover made, getting it listed on Amazon and/or my own website, doing some marketing for it, getting the word out, setting some goals for sales figures, and finally getting it published. I would also want to consider the impact I wanted on people and what the book would do for me in my mind other than simply be a hobby or provide some income.

The point is that I had the general idea of writing a book, but my own ability to create a process was not ideal and took far too long. Even when I started getting input from authors through other books or on podcasts or webinars, I found it very difficult to have the daily discipline required and know the next steps or what to do when challenges arise in order to get the book written. Some how-to books for authoring let you know the chunking down theory of writing a book. They inform you of how many words to write in total, how many to write in a day, and how long that should take.

The best single piece of advice that worked for me came from Chandler Bolt's *Book Launch* book. He suggested that I commit to just getting a first draft done and don't worry about the final book or marketing yet. That was the key to getting this book into your hands. Most "how-to-write-a-book" books are similar in their process. But now I'd found one that added just that one extra element that got me on the right track. It was a better process, at least for me. I then decided to simply follow the process Chandler advocates in his book and deliver the result I was looking for.

So perhaps I would have been better off 10 years ago having a book-writing coach who set out a plan or schedule, kept me on track and pushed me toward the goal. I could have been done in 3, 6, 9 or 12 *months,* rather than 10 years. Because writing the book hasn't taken 10 years. Writing the first draft took less than two months. Even that didn't take as much time as it sounds.

The first draft was achieved by writing 30-60 minutes per day. Writing at a pace of 1,000 words per hour meant that in 30-60 days I would have the first draft of a 30,000 to 60,000-word book completed. With the average non-fiction book being around 50,000 words, I was in the right range. Editing and market preparation has taken a further two months. And the actual launch preparation took a further one month. Think of how many more books I could have written in that 10-year period if I had had somebody else help push me through the barriers (my own mental barriers! That I hadn't even realized were there.). They could have helped me get the book written, published, and marketed. In addition, think of how many hundreds or thousands of people who could have been helped with this information and my perspective in that time frame. Well, *now* is the second-best time to achieve anything. And *now* here it is in your hands.

So you need to have a clear outcome in mind. Get moving toward that outcome. Adjust your own actions to improve initial results. Seek further assistance from other successful people, especially in the area you are looking to succeed in. Have a finish line so you know when you are done with that stage or project. Then continue on while seeking ever-improving methods to improve the results you are getting. Keep with this program and you will shift to being unstoppable.

I. Fixed and growth

A key element in thinking about your mindset is whether it can change. In her best-selling book, *Mindset*, Carol S. Dweck, PhD., a world-renowned Stanford University psychologist, looks into this deeply. She notes that there are two types of mindset: fixed and growth.

Someone with a fixed mindset will believe that their intelligence, abilities, and talents are fixed or unchangeable. People who have a growth mindset believe that their talents, intelligence, and abilities are malleable and can improve with effort, training, and discipline.

When you have a fixed mindset, you don't try very hard to change because you start from the idea that you can't change what you were born with. In contrast, the growth mindset is curious and interested in change that is positive and useful. Additionally, since the person believes they can improve, they begin the process and then see results. These results confirm that improvements can be made and this encouraging proof motivates the person to progress further.

Remarkably, you can have a fixed mindset for many aspects of life while having a growth mindset for several others, all simultaneously. For example, you may have a fixed mindset with respect to your ability to drive a car: you assume you are as good as you can be. At the same time, you have a growth mindset and enthusiasm for online marketing and are reading about it and taking a course next month to further improve.

What I would like you to take away from this section is that you can improve anything in your life. I am sure you are already improving in some areas such as at work, or with your health and fitness. Even if it is with small steps and just a little progress, it is still progress and improvement. So listen to yourself speak about things you could do. If you hear "I can't" or "I'm not," then stop yourself and understand why you are thinking that. I am sure it isn't because you actually aren't able to improve by taking a course or following a process. It may simply be that you have a fixed mindset for that part of your identity. A simple shift is all you need.

Cultivate a growth mindset in all aspects of your life. It would be unusual if you could not be better or not refine your thoughts on anything in your life. Be confident about where you are but be curious about where you could be in all areas of your life. Open your mind to endless possibilities. Wonder what it could look like. Sign up to a course. Read a book on the topic. Watch a documentary or YouTube channel created by a beginner or an expert in that field.

Book 20 minutes into your diary now. This time will be for you to search online, find, and read or watch something new today. Use any topic you find interesting and would like to know more about so you can improve. Start training your growth mindset.

II. Programming challenges and fun
Don't Stop Me Now

We can be our own worst enemy. Our self-talk and certain learned phrases that are "programmed" into us can hold us back. We hear many phrases from our parents, grandparents, and teachers as well as people on television, radio, and the internet. Just because someone says something, or it is common to hear in our peer group, does not mean it is true or helpful.

Part of the challenge is that many of those words that you have heard repeatedly throughout your life you have accepted as true, as immutable facts. So regardless of whether you are 20 or 50 years old, you will have heard certain phrases so often you may even say them without giving them a second thought. You should consider those thoughts and see who believes the opposite or at least can provide an alternate point of view.

Be careful when you hear yourself say or even think things such as:

"I could never do that."
"I can't."
"It's alright for some."
"I don't want to be rich."
"I've always been..."

Saying these types of things, along with many other similarly negative phrases, will not help you achieve anything.

You need to break out of that fixed mindset and go for growth. Take some area of your life that you have wanted to change for a little while now and decide to improve it. Commit to beginning a process that might lead to the change, or outcome, that you would enjoy in your life.

For example, if you would like to slim down a little or get a little fitter, start right now and go for a 15-minute walk. I'm serious. Put down the book now and go. It will be here when you get back. You'll feel great having accomplished a step toward your new life already.

Just start with a walk or short run if that's what gets you going. You don't have to think about running a marathon. Though that could be an Outrageous goal (we cover that in more depth in chapter 10). Just get outside and walk 7 minutes in one direction and 7 minutes back. If you can do that, you can do it again. Then prove that you can go 10 minutes each way. Alternatively, try to cover the 15-minute distance in 14 minutes. Have some fun with this stage. Change things up or do different things. The key is to begin a process that moves you in the direction you need to go.

Now sometimes there will be times when you won't want to follow through on your new activity. You may be feeling low on energy, overwhelmed, held back or complacent. If so, do something to change your state of mind and your physical state. Use a song, video, quote, or visualization to bring you through the challenging moment and rev you up for another round. One song I've been using more recently is Queen's *Don't Stop Me Now*. I'll recite a few of the lyrics and feel the music building inside of me. If I need to take a break, I will play this song during that time and really get into it. I always feel more positive, energized, and ready to go, go, go.

III. Something for the pain
The ER Gap (Expectation v Reality)

One of the more common causes of distress in life occurs when our expectations for our life aren't met by our reality, in the anticipated timeframe. The greater the gap between your expectations and your reality, then the greater the stress, unhappiness, and depression you may experience. It is great to have expectations and to keep making them more challenging. However, you should allow reality to meet your expectations and celebrate each time that occurs.

Once reality has met your expectations, it is useful to cast your line out again and aim for a new, challenging target. By raising your expectations throughout your life, you should continue to progress.

A word of caution though. Should you regress in some way, be sure to adjust your expectations or it will cause undue distress.

An example of this would be the following:

You have been working hard at your job and have been advised of an imminent promotion with a commensurate salary increase. However, a recent drop in demand disrupts your company's growth plan and you're suddenly laid off. You are probably best to readjust your expectations from having a promotion and a raise to the reality of simply finding a comparable new job. Certainly don't spend the promotion money you thought you were about to receive. Get yourself back in the game with your new job and adjusted reality and set new expectations from there with appropriate timeframes.

Remember, the higher your expectations are above your reality, the more stress you will feel. So you can help manage the stress by keeping an eye on the ER Gap.

You can reduce your stress and maintain higher levels of calm and happiness by doing some of the following:

- Set realistic expectations given the timeframe. Bigger expectations usually require longer timeframes.
- Set smaller milestone targets that you can achieve more frequently. You'll build momentum and the milestones will act as checkpoints to keep you on track for your longer-term expectations.
- Set some easy and incredible goals to create both certainty and excitement in your goal-setting. We explore this concept further in chapter 10 as we review the MTO goal-setting method.
- Keep your expectations low and your hopes high. This way your reality should be better than your expectations. You may find you are more grateful and pleased with your life while still working towards goals and having hope for a better life.

Pain now or pain later

Most of us want good times now *and* later. Unfortunately, that is not usually how it works. The universe is in balance. So every action has an equal and opposite reaction.

"We must all suffer one of two pains: the pain of discipline or the pain of regret."

– Jim Rohn

Now ideally you will enjoy the work you do. But it is often the case that we do not enjoy all aspects of our chosen work and certainly not all of the time. So, given that, it seems there will be days where we will have pain that we need to overcome. What Jim is saying, in the quote above, is that you will need to push through and be disciplined and suffer the pain now so you can enjoy the benefits later.

You see, of the two pains, discipline is much lighter to carry than regret. There is no need to test this theory for yourself though by waiting 10 years. Simply ask people who are 10 or 20 years older than you are now. If they are being honest with you, you will usually hear the weight of their regret in their words or voice. Fortunately, you still have plenty of time to change the ending of your story.

"Twenty years from now, you will be more disappointed by the things that you didn't do than by the ones you did do. So throw off the bow lines. Sail away from the safe harbor. Catch the trade winds in your sails. Explore. Dream. Discover."

– Mark Twain

Short term v long term - Enjoy now or enjoy later

"Today I will do what others won't so tomorrow I can do what others can't."

– Jerry Rice

If we constantly feed our short-term desires, we are unlikely to achieve our goals in life. Short-term desires tend to be enjoyable, fun, and distracting from the work we need to do. With a longer-term outlook, you are more likely to say no to the extra scoop of ice cream today so you can enjoy being slimmer in a few months, or no to another night out this week so you can save for a house and enjoy your new home.

In the short term, we can see how everything matters. From speeding, to binge eating or drinking, to studying for exams or not. In the longer term, you might think such things are less important when you consider decades of life. In the very long term, it can be hard to tell what was important and made a difference. This is often a tough concept to get our heads around. So some people take the long-term view that nothing really matters and apply it to the short term and continuously act undisciplined and inappropriately.

However, if we made everything in the moment very important, we might drive ourselves crazy with all of the competing priorities. For example, in the next hour, we might want to work to make money for food, but also spend time with our children or a sick relative, or simply have a break for ourselves. It all seems important.

"I hated every minute of training, but I said, 'Don't quit. Suffer now and live the rest of your life as a champion."

– Muhammad Ali

In contrast, our actions may have a significant effect on things in the distant future, but it will be hard to trace it all back 100 years from now.

Be careful with your words when saying you will do something later. Precision is important. If you say you will do something later, be clear on when later is exactly. Is it 30 minutes from now? One year? Four years? 10 years? 40 years? It's amazing how things that are put off for a short time can be left undone for a very long time. That is the Law of Diminishing Intent in action. We will cover this law in more detail in chapter 14.

IV. The power of the mind

"Our deepest fear is not that we are inadequate. Our deepest fear is that we are powerful beyond measure. It is our light, not our darkness, that most frightens us."

– Marianne Williamson

Think about the mind for a moment. Can you point to it like you do your leg? Your brain is in your head and you can see that in pictures. Have you ever seen a picture of a mind?

The mind is the power behind thought, emotion, consciousness, imagination, perception, memory, instinct, judgment, and language. Read those over again, slowly, and think about whether you can see them or touch them. It is a strange thing. Where do thoughts originate? Where does instinct come from? What about consciousness?

These are questions you can research separately and have fun with wrapping your head around. There are different theories and ideas out there which you can follow and explore. You may agree with one and settle on it. And you may change your mind at some point after that.

When I reflect on the mind, its strikes me how extremely powerful it is. It has created the most wonderful things and the most horrible. In fact, your mind or someone else's has been responsible for everything made by people. It is responsible for all cultures, religions, perspectives, and physical items such as cars, phones, houses, medicines, airplanes, and weapons.

An argument for the mind's incredible power is that people have created the computer but no computer has yet created a human.

Your mind is like a super-computing, heat-seeking missile. Everything will be processed literally and in order, so be clear in your thinking, communication, and action. Of course, you can change the target coordinates if you need to later on but try to focus on the outcome you want. This is where the real power is.

In addition, be careful with what you visualize and what you emulate. Everything has an influence on you. Even if you think it doesn't or won't, it will. So, you should be precise in your use of words and mental imagery. You will attract, and be attracted to, that which lingers in your mind.

Finally, you can train this super powerful machine in your brain. That is the best news of all. Just like you can train for a sport or prepare for a test, you can build these powerful thoughts and actions that we've touched on into your life. You may find it a bit difficult, or uncomfortable, at first, especially if you are already hard-wired in a different way or have a fixed mindset for this. Simply add to your ability each day. Make it a "must-do" action until it is a habit. Set milestones and keep improving. In three months, six months and 12 months, you will be noticing the difference. Stick with it. That is the key to all success. Persistent discipline. You will begin to see from this focus and consistent action that you start to shift from uncomfortable on your way to being an unstoppable force.

KEY POINTS

CHAPTER 2 – MINDSET

- Master your mind and you can master anything.

- Give up the story of your life so you can create the life story that you want.

- Be crystal clear in your thoughts and precise with your words and actions.

- Changes come from the thoughts you develop in your mind.

- Your daily thoughts and actions determine your daily outcomes.

- Worrying is like praying for bad stuff to happen. Focus on great outcomes.

- Seek better methods to improve the results you are getting.

- You can improve anything in your life.

- Be aware of the expectation v reality gap – readjust accordingly.

- Discipline is lighter to carry than regret.

- If we constantly feed our short-term desires, we are unlikely to achieve our longer-term goals in life. Be disciplined for the long-term.

- Everything has an influence on you. Be mindful of what you see and hear.

- Your mind is an incredibly powerful tool. Use it well.

STEP 1

ACTIONS... TO HELP YOU *THINK*

- ▸ Dream more and visualize your exceptional future.

- ▸ Find the right finish for you. Write down what you would love and also what others want for you. Reflect on both lists.

- ▸ Imagine the most exciting and fascinating future possible for yourself. Write it down. Now get to work on it!

- ▸ Write down and reflect on what you want today and compare this to what you wanted in your youth.

- ▸ What did you want to do in life that got you excited?

- ▸ How did you want to live?

- ▸ Think about your years from 8-18 for inspiration.

- ▸ Answer the questions from Chapter 1 at the end of sub-section II. (see page 5)

- ▸ Plan the detail. Write, draw or dictate. Planning makes you think ahead.

- ▸ Adjust your own current actions to improve initial results.

- ▸ Seek further assistance from other successful people, especially in the area you are looking to succeed in. Ask them questions or if they can help you in a specific way.

- ▸ Have a finish line so you know when you are done with that stage or project. Then keep going while seeking better methods to continually improve the results you are getting.

> Make it a "must-do" action until it is a habit. Set milestones and keep improving. In three months, six months and 12 months, you will notice the difference.

> Stick with it. That is the key to all success. Persistent discipline.

> Like the mime in the box, mentally move the mental barriers you've created in your life.

> Use visualization techniques and exposure therapy. Start considering some alternative-you scenarios. Sit with these and get comfortable with them.

> Write out a 'hoping but not happening' list for your life. Consider a different process for each one.

> Make an 'Absolutely Don't Want' list.

> Make an 'Absolutely Do Want' list.

> Seek some independent, external feedback to accurately assess where you are.

> Cultivate a growth mindset in all aspects of your life. Ask yourself, "How can I improve?" for each specific area of your life.

STEP 2 - **OVERCOME**

You may now know where you want to be. But you are not there yet. And that is ok. Awareness of the outcome you want is the first step. Now we need to understand why you are not there already. What is it that you need to overcome to reach your dream?

Usually, when we are not where we want to be yet, it is because we are not clear in our thinking or not following the best, precise actions to deliver those results. Having grown up on a dairy farm, I learned this early on in life.

You reap what you sow. If you plant corn, don't expect potatoes to grow. Equally, if you plant in the autumn instead of the spring, you shouldn't expect much of a crop at harvest time. In addition, plant more than you will need, as some seeds won't deliver. They could be eaten, rot, dry out or many other things. Understand that we need to be clear in what we want to harvest, plant well, time it well, prepare for challenges, and tend to the garden every day.

Think about what might be holding you back in these terms. Have you clearly outlined precisely what you would like to achieve? Are you planting the right seeds? Are you putting in the right amount of time and effort? Are you making progress every day? Is your life improving? Do keep in mind that while preparing the land, planting the seeds and encouraging the crops, you are unlikely to see much, if any, evidence of progress. You need to believe in the process.

You may know what you need to overcome. And you may not. You may have no clue. That is what this chapter is for. It is to help you identify the challenges you need to overcome. It will also help you remove the obstacles, reframe your thinking, improve your actions, and set a clear route to success.

There are many ingredients that go into a stew, and many elements in creating your you.

You may find some of these thoughts challenging. You may want to stop. But don't. We are shifting from the uncomfortable to the unstoppable and self-awareness is critical in moving forward and making progress. Just as we made the effort and improvements during school years, say from year 4 to year 5, you need to do this work, and be clear, so you can build on your knowledge. It is not always easy or comfortable but it will help you dramatically. You will get used to playing at a higher level. You can do it!

Chapter 3. Current beliefs, ideas, thoughts

What are your beliefs? Have you given it much thought?

Did you inherit them from parents?

Did you buy them at the newsstand?

Did you overhear them on the tv, a podcast, or YouTube?

Beliefs are very important in your life. Consider what they are and why you have those particular ones. Ask if they fit with the world we live in and how you want to feel.

A belief is simply a confidence that something exits, or is true, without requiring proof. You may believe kindness is important, fire is a useful element, and sunshine is better than rain. You might also believe that you can't sing well, aren't good at math, or could not give a speech in front of thousands of people. You may even believe you are a good dancer, loyal friend, and a fabulous cook. There are even some people that believe the US has never landed on the Moon and the Earth is flat. Your beliefs are up to you. No one can force you to change them or explain them. However, changing your beliefs can completely change your life. Your future truly is in your hands.

Oddly enough, humans feel something first, an emotion, and then create a belief. Then they tend to go find data and perspectives to back up the way they feel. For example, you might think, "I am afraid to speak in front of the class." Fear is the emotion. You may then feel you shouldn't speak and then believe you are not very good at it. Often, you will then find one or two data points to back this up, such as the time you spoke up and everybody laughed. You may not recall the 20 times you have spoken up and all went fine. You could have accessed those memories and that data, but you were looking to confirm your new belief. Your mind will find the data to confirm your beliefs whether that is good for you or not. Remember, your mind is like a computer. It carries out orders without discretion. So be careful what you ask it to do!

Although we create some of our own beliefs, a great many of them have been learned or bought from someone else. We absorb them from our parents, caregivers, and grandparents when we are young. Then we are influenced by our teachers and peers through our school days. Subsequently, we are influenced by our colleagues, industry, and chosen religion. Throughout your life you will also be influenced by other people who convey their beliefs to you via books, radio, television, the internet, movies, and social media. Be selective with your money because what you buy shapes your beliefs whether you want it to or not. This is the downside of exposure therapy. The more you expose yourself to harmful or unhelpful commentary or beliefs, the more they became familiar to you. Then you may start to accept those views and relate better to others who communicate those views. So be careful and selective with what you see, hear, say, and think. Make sure your knowledge consumption is positive, empowering, and objectively challenged.

Beliefs can change throughout our lives. What our parents believe may be what we believe for some time. However, we may change that belief. Even still, we may change that belief again at a later date. Knowing that beliefs are malleable confirms that we can overcome or change any beliefs that are holding us back. Challenge any belief you have that makes you uncomfortable.

If you inherited a record player or fax machine from your parents, you may want to consider the value of those items to you. Sure there will be sentimental attachment because they belonged to your parents. However, they may not be very useful to you in the world of today. Consider the usefulness value that these items represent to you and what other devices you could find to support your life better. Just like beliefs, you do not need to accept hand-me-downs. Traditions can be great to uphold, but not if they go against your values. Inquire, be curious, listen to other people and your heart, while also considering your head. Don't be afraid to move on to the next level and leave unhelpful beliefs behind.

I. Fear – The great barrier belief

"Our greatest fear should not be of failure ... but of succeeding at things in life that don't really matter."

– Francis Chan

There are many ideas about what hold people back from achieving the goals that they want. However, the biggest brake you will have on your future success, and speed of development, will be fear. Fear is a funny topic. Generally, people don't like to think of themselves as having fear. Although without fear, you can't have bravery or courage, which is the act of overcoming fear. Remember, fear is a natural survival mechanism to protect you from unknown outcomes and potentially painful situations, animals, and people.

There are many different ways to look at fear. And there are many different types of fear. We will look at a few of these right now.

Some people look at fear as being non-existent, such as, "The only thing we have to fear is fear itself." This modern quote is usually attributed to Franklin D. Roosevelt.

Then there is the brand/slogan "no fear." This slogan seems to indicate that you should just walk out there and keep fear out of your mind or have no fear at all.

Additionally, there was a book released in 1987 by Susan Jeffers entitled, *Feel the Fear and Do it Anyway*. This title is referring to the idea that some level of fear always exists in our minds and can be difficult to block out. For those of you struggling with that challenge, your best option is to feel the fear and do it anyway. It is in doing the thing you are fearful of that you find your courage. It allows you to be brave and overcome a difficult or uncomfortable situation.

So what is fear exactly? It is simply a mental survival mechanism. Our minds don't force us to think one way or another, but our habits tend to lead us to believe that either the unhappy ending, or the happy one, is more likely to occur. The mind creates scenarios where outcomes are unknown, highlighting how these situations can be damaging, painful, or deadly. Fearful thinking then alerts us to stop and take notice of the situation. For many, the negative/protective mind wins the battle and stops us from progressing.

Most people don't even get to the part where they would assess the situation. If they did, this is where they would consider whether more information was required to make the decision or if the mind had any rational justification for what it was projecting on the big screen in our head. The mind is continually playing fascinating dramas on our internal Jumbotron. Not only do we see it on our big screen but before that we usually feel it in our body in the way we vibrate. Opposite to how The Beach Boys would sing, "I'm picking up good vibrations," you will actually be picking up negative vibrations. These subtle fear vibrations provide you with the seed of concern and soon your random and worst-case thoughts will help to convince you to not go ahead with whatever it was you wanted to do. You must allow yourself to be uncomfortable as you begin the shift along the continuum to unstoppable.

Once again, this fear is there to protect the individual or animal. While protection is a survival instinct, it is not so helpful with growth. However, we can use it to grow by understanding what specifically is making us fearful and sitting with that emotion and coming to terms with it. This will allow us to more quickly shift into growth mindset and move beyond the challenging situation that we find ourselves stuck in (which is our own mental block — not something or someone). We then need to get comfortable in our head and our being as we begin to take action in the physical world.

Remember the fear you have may not be the fear someone else has. It has a lot to do with perception, which draws from our own learning, experiences, and exposure. For example, fire is fire. It is not necessarily good or bad. However, one person may be afraid of fire because it ravaged their childhood home and nearly took them with it. Therefore, they may see fire as bad or something to be fearful of. Another person, without that experience, but whose family used fire to keep the house warm during long, cold winters will appreciate fire and how it helped them survive. Therefore, they may see fire as good. So how you perceive something is just how it is filtered through your lens. Your perception comes from a specific situation in time reflected through your unique experience, knowledge, and philosophy.

Try this exercise. Think of a situation that makes you anxious or uncomfortable, like touching spiders or public speaking. Got it? Make a brief note of it now so you don't forget. There are some very common situations that make people uncomfortable. So, if you can't think of one on your own that's personal to you, I will now give you a few options and see if one of these makes you feel anxious or uncomfortable.

- Having to phone someone you don't know or don't know very well.
- Having to sit next to somebody that you have not met before on a long journey.
- Having a snake slither over your bare arms and legs.
- Asking for a raise at work.
- Confronting someone, especially in authority.
- Worry about or fearing something bad happening.
- Fear of flying.

Reflect, rehearse and visualize

Take one of these, or the one that you have already got in your head, and just sit down and reflect on it. It's not actually happening to you. You're not on a plane. You don't have an animal or snake crawling on you. You don't need to call someone that you're uncomfortable calling. This is just a mental exercise. So, let's treat it as such. There is nothing to get concerned about. Nothing to worry about. You can relax with these thoughts. Let's just get inside our mind and see why it's making us uncomfortable. Maybe then we can understand what that motivation is and how we might deal with it.

So just sit and think about being in that situation. If you want to push the boundary now, let's get a step closer to the actual situation by using our imagination. So, imagine you are at the airport and you are about to go through security to get on your airplane. How does this make you feel?

Go through it step by step to see what part of it you are getting the emotional reaction from. Once you can understand where the main fear point is, you can go back to it and reduce its impact on you over time. Eventually, you could have trained your mind to accept a little bit of discomfort around your fear or even rebrand that negative vibration to excitement. Of course, you may want to get some professional help to work through any extreme fears, but this simple exercise could get you started or help with some more common fears.

"The mind is its own place, and in itself can make a heaven of hell, a hell of heaven"

– John Milton

II. Money challenges

Money can be such a contentious issue. Many people do not like to talk about money itself. Talking about it can be perceived as rude, inappropriate, flashy, and vulgar. However, money is an essential element in our modern world. So, it may be one topic you should start to get more comfortable around.

You see, your beliefs about money impact quite a lot of your life. It impacts your career, livelihood, holidays, food, politics, friends, business success, retirement, housing, neighborhood, who you get your news from, where you live, education, and your spouse or partner. And that is just to name a few of the many things where money affects us. So, if your perception of money is not very good or helpful, we should address this now, overcome it, and begin on a more empowering road.

Everything you think and feel about money has been learned by you. In fact, everything you currently believe you have decided on and you want to believe. Like my fire analogy above. You can see money however you want. Money is just money. It is you who holds the judgment about it and about the people with or without it. So, are your thoughts about money supporting you in the best way possible? Are your beliefs about money allowing you maximum joy?

You see, if you want more money in your life, just like friends, you need to attract it by being attractive. Being attractive means speaking highly of it, as you would a person you wanted as a friend. It means saying good things about who it associates with. A friend won't stick around for long if you keep putting down all the people they associate with. Well, neither will money. For clarification, it may be a little less about money choosing, like a person would, to stay away from you, and more about your antipathy and you pushing it and related items away from you.

Some phrases and beliefs people have about money that have a negative connotation are fairly well known. I'll list a few of them here:

"She is filthy rich."

"Money is the root of all evil."

"Money doesn't grow on trees."

"If they have money, they must have done something illegal, immoral, or crooked."

"I'd rather be happy than rich."

"Money can't buy happiness."

If you say any of these, please stop. They are not helpful. Having a negative mindset about anything is not helpful, but especially money. Develop a neutral or positive mindset about money. Why choose to be negative about it, when a positive viewpoint will, if nothing else, keep you in a better mood. In addition, you are more likely to attract money if you say nicer things about it and the people who have it. That is just the way it is.

"Money is usually attracted, not pursued."

– Jim Rohn

If you want to earn more money, become a money magnet. Do things so well that people want to pay you for it. The better you are at giving (value), the more you will be receiving (money). It's an odd twist in the universe but it works out quite well for people. Once you know how these things work, you can have them work for you and not against you.

III. Challenge your Why

Why are you going to spend your time, energy, and thoughts on your dreams or specific goal? Presumably the answer is so that you can feel great! Now feeling great can be a tricky thing. Sometimes we think we're going to feel great when something happens, and we do. Sometimes we think we will feel great when we achieve something, and we don't. This comes down to a number of things. Some of the key components are:

- Why you wanted the result in the first place.
- What your original expectations were.
- How you went about it.
- How long it took to achieve.
- What you had to sacrifice or give up to achieve the goal.

Although it doesn't seem to make a lot of sense that achieving one of your goals won't make you feel good, it is actually true that it can happen. Have you ever wanted something to eat, for example, perhaps some sort of treat? Then you go along and get that item. It could be a chocolate bar or a big dessert, like a large piece of cake. Now the reason you may not feel great after having what you thought you wanted could be that this is at odds with your values or a higher goal, which might be more important. It's not ideal if you have been trying to reduce your weight or get fit, and you've been doing really well, but then you eat two pieces of cake and feel like you have blown it. If you believe your diet (higher goal) has been jeopardized, then you may not feel so great about yourself or your discipline. A short-term desire, at odds with your longer-term goal, feels good in the moment, but the disappointment grows as time goes on. Recall the earlier phrase about the pain of discipline or the pain of regret.

Another time this happens is when we're looking at things on the internet, in the newspaper, or at the shops and we come across something that we think we would really like. This might be an item of clothing or something as big as a car or house. Sometimes we act impulsively and go ahead and buy that thing we feel we want. This is when consumer dissonance sets in and just after we buy it, we think this doesn't actually make us feel good for some reason. Maybe we haven't done enough research. Maybe we think we need to have spoken to somebody else before making the purchase. Sometimes we think it's a waste of money or we've spent money we didn't even have. This is how buying something we think we want (in the moment) can actually leave us feeling guilty or sad rather than feeling great.

If we want to feel great about a purchase, or a situation, it is often best to understand why we want what we want and really get clear on how it's going to bring joy to our life. Sometimes we think buying that new gadget, going out for an amazing dinner, taking a "must-do" holiday, or spending a night out with our fabulous friends is going to give us that great feeling we are looking for. However, sometimes we just act on impulse, or the memories of those things feeling great in the past, and we don't take into account how we have changed in our thinking over time. When we really dig deep, sometimes these things seem like a great idea but actually have a number of downsides that, when weighed up in totality, indicate that these are not the best choices overall.

"So tell me what you want, what you really, really want."

– Spice Girls

We humans are very quick to forget how badly we wanted something, especially soon after we have it. This can happen immediately after we've gotten what we wanted, but sometimes it can take days, weeks, or months. Occasionally it's got to exit our life before we truly appreciate it or miss it. You may have heard the phrase, "you don't know what you've got, till it's gone." It is so true. If you want to put that to a tune, you should stream the 80s power rocking band Cinderella, who put out a song with a similar title.

Get your motor running, but will it stall?

After a few years of living and working in London, I can remember wanting to buy a car. Ideally it would be a convertible sports car. I was thinking of something sporty and fun with a bit of power for my wife and me to go exploring down quintessential English country lanes. I secured a test drive for an MX-5 first as the dealer was very close to our house. Then my wife got a call back from the dealer and they suggested a new «innocent blue," limited edition, 10th anniversary MX-5. She seemed excited and as this was going to be mainly for her to get to and from work, we went to see it straight away. Before the test drive was over, my wife was sold and said, "I want this car." So we bought it.

It was in perfect condition, so we were quite precious with that new car when we first drove it on our way home. So precious, in fact, that my wife wanted to pull over and let me drive, as she didn't want to be the first one to get a mark on it. Well, I didn't want to put a mark on it either, but somebody had to drive us home! I gently eased into the driver's seat and, almost immediately on moving, I knocked the tyre against the curb and put a tiny scratch on the hubcap. Yikes! Although it was tense for a minute or two, we got over it fairly quickly and moved on.

Although we loved that car and treated it very well, I can remember times when we just took it for granted. Sometimes we would forget how much we had wanted it, how fortunate we were to be able to afford the cost of owning and running it, and the sheer joy we felt zipping around with the top down and the wind in our hair: especially on the small lanes in the English countryside. After a while, we would sometimes forget how it used to make us feel. At times it became just a mode of transport, a luxury and even an administrative hassle (MOT, insurance, break in, repairs, etc.).

Then one day, we decided we wanted to go traveling around the world for a year. We figured it was time to sell that car. After we sold it, we realized once again how much joy and fun that car brought us. We had overcome the initial concern about scratching the car but also sometimes let its ownership be commonplace. To ensure you are feeling great as often as possible, remember to enjoy the newness and move quickly past concerns. Also, appreciate things just as much after some time has passed as you did before or in the early days of having it.

"Don't know what you've got, until it's gone."

– Cinderella

I've explored several ideas or themes with a car in mind. However, if you stop and think about it, they are as appropriate for relationships, jobs, houses, health and family. Decide on your current, strong Why. Write down what you really, really want. Appreciate all that you have now, every day, instead of waiting until it is gone to miss it. Use the good china. Don't save and protect the good things for only that one moment in the future. Use it day to day, or frequently at least, and enjoy it each time.

We humans are also very adaptable. As soon as we get over something (Overcome!) which was challenging, or scared us a little, we move on. Like putting the first little scratch on the car. Frequently we even slap a bravery badge or pride sticker on it, or inflate our chest a little and say, "It was nothing." So we can turn something that we were not going to enjoy into something that we can be proud of and reflect back on fondly. Be proud of the scars, dents, setbacks and all the other issues you've had to overcome. With a strong Why, you'll happily know it was worth it. So just keep moving forward.

Right. So now we have explored why you might be reading this book. You probably want something in your life to change, to make your life better. You may even have thought through what that is and some of the hurdles you will need to overcome. So now we need to go about making it happen. This will bring us to our next section of the book and the following chapters. Get ready, as we will now focus on some mindset tactics to diminish the impact from the obstacles that will invariably get in our way.

IV. Map out how to remove, detour around or change beliefs

If you are going to succeed in shifting from uncomfortable to unstoppable, you will need some thoughts and strategies to get past your own beliefs. It sounds fairly easy but it can be more involved and challenging than you first think. Ask anyone who has tried to quit smoking, get fit, or make more money. It can be a real struggle, even though the reality of each sounds so simple: don't buy cigarettes, eat less and move more, and provide more value to more people than you do now.

Let's start off with a three-step process for you to think about.

- First you need to confront the brutal reality of what you think, feel, and believe.

- Second you need to be honest about whether these thoughts, feelings, and beliefs serve you as well as other thoughts, feelings, and beliefs might.
- Third you need to assess and understand what thoughts, feelings, and beliefs you would like to move forward with into the next chapter of your life. And which ones you would like to leave behind.

For example, perhaps you would like to make more money but feel bad and uncomfortable about making even more than others who have far less money than you do already. You need to use the three-step process above and confront those thoughts, be honest about whether they serve you well, and decide which thoughts to move forward with. Oftentimes we have simply absorbed certain ways of thinking from our environment. This might include our parents, a teacher, family, friends, co-workers, the newspaper we read, or our favorite tv or radio show. Stop and peel back a few layers. Understand what the thoughts are and see what alternatives there are out there. You may find helpful phrases and ideas from unfamiliar places. The idea below may help you with the Money Challenges section above.

Being poor doesn't help poor people any more than sleeping alone on the street helps the homeless.

Have empathy, of course. But do not live their existence. If you have more strength, power, wealth, or persuasion than they do, then use it for your benefit as well as their benefit and for the benefit of others. You could earn more money by providing greater value to the marketplace, which is a good thing. In addition, some of your higher income will go to taxes which will aim to help the community. Moreover, you could use a portion of that extra income to donate to a charity that helps the less-well-off in your community or farther afield. Always try to build people up, in whatever way that you can, and that includes yourself.

Removing a limiting belief is a great start toward developing a better mindset and helping you overcome your current mindset challenges. Instead of saying, "She is filthy rich," you could simply stop commenting on people you don't know everything about. You will rarely know what the financial position of others is. They may have a nice house or a fancy car, but they may also be one week away from being foreclosed on or having the car repossessed. Not everything is as you perceive it to be.

To **detour around** a limiting belief, you need to stay away from it. This may mean that you distance yourself a little from friends who aren't on this journey with you. Or if you find yourself in a conversation where negative words are being spoken, do not engage with it. Simply listen and try not to respond with words or body language. Even better would be to walk away.

A quick way to **change** limiting beliefs is to write down the opposite and look at it several times per day. Repetition is the key to learning anything. Whether it is your times tables, or the spelling of someone's name, repetition will help to lodge it in your memory. So instead of saying "Money is the root of all evil," you could write down, "Money accelerates exciting things into my life."

KEY POINTS

CHAPTER 3 – CURRENT BELIEFS, IDEAS, THOUGHTS

> ‣ Awareness of the outcome you want is the first step. You also need to understand why you are not there.

> ‣ Changing your beliefs can completely change your life.

- Your mind is like a computer. Be aware of what you are asking it to do! And what information you consume.

- Feel your fear and do it anyway.

- Do not let the protective mind win and stop you from progressing (If it is safe to do so)

- Allow yourself to be uncomfortable. Get comfortable with that feeling.

- How you perceive something is just how it is filtered through your own unique lens.

- Understand where your main fear point is. The aim is to address it and reduce its impact on you over time.

- Have a neutral or positive mindset towards money – attract it!

- A short-term desire, at odds with your longer-term goal, feels good in the moment, but the disappointment grows as time goes on. Recall the earlier phrase about the pain of discipline or the pain of regret.

- If you want to feel great about a purchase or situation, it is often best to understand why you want it and be clear on why you think it will bring longer-term joy to your life.

- Always build people up, in whatever way you can.

- Remove, detour around or change your limiting beliefs as soon as you can.

Chapter 4. Regret: Woulda, coulda, shoulda

Recall from chapter two that we will all suffer the pain of discipline or the pain of regret. Well, these are the three pillars of regret. These are a few words which we sometimes say to ourselves that usually just bring regret into our lives. Try to resist thinking or speaking these words. Replace them with more powerful, forward-looking words or phrases, such as, "The next time X happens, I will..." or "I know I can do Y better in the future if I ..." or "I'm going to...".

"Woulda" or "Would have" often means that you wanted to do something but you were hesitant or unaware for some reason. For example, "I would have stopped their argument but I wasn't sure it was my place to get involved" (Hesitant). Or "I would have bought your plane ticket for Mom's birthday if I had made myself aware of why you weren't going to make it" (Unaware).

"Coulda" or "Could have" usually means you were aware and capable of doing something but chose not to do it. For example, "I could have stopped their argument from escalating out of control but decided it was their disagreement to resolve." (Regret for not affecting the outcome).

"Shoulda" or Should have" will frequently mean you were aware, you were capable and you chose not to, but you really wish now that you had. It is especially painful if you believe your actions would have delivered an outcome different from the one that occurred. For example, "I should have stopped their argument. I didn't think one of them would end up in the hospital." (Regret for not affecting a bad outcome).

Be aware of these words and the sentiment they convey. When you hear them in your mind or mouth, say, "Woah, choose better words." Switch those words out and practice using more empowering, future-oriented phrases as noted above.

I. Let bygones be

One of the worst things you can do to yourself is to continually remind yourself of the mistakes you think you made. You also don't want to punish yourself for things that have happened, whether they were in your control or not.

You will be better off if you leave the past in the past. Learn to move on and look forward to a better future. You can learn from your past, but only take the lesson with you. Leave the pain, second-guessing and challenges behind. Those burdens will become too heavy to carry everywhere with you.

You have probably heard the phrase, forgive and forget. It's a powerful phrase that seems so simple, yet for many of us, it is hard to follow. It is hard to forget something if you have not accepted it. But once you accept that it has happened, it is easier to move on. You may even forgive the person as they may be having harder challenges in life than you. The sooner you accept it happened and forgive the person, the sooner you can move forward and forget about it. Your mind won't need to spend any more time thinking about revenge, or what could have been or how you were unjustly treated. Get closure and move on.

If you don't do this, it may eat away at you. Meanwhile, the other person will be out dancing. So, who are you really punishing?

I was amazed to see a Larry King Live clip where he was interviewing former US President Ronald Reagan. It's a 3-minute clip. In it, President Reagan noted that he forgave the man who tried to assassinate him. And the man almost succeeded.

He managed to get a bullet within an inch of the President's heart. President Reagan said that he had even added him to his prayers as the man probably needed it, as he clearly had some challenges. President Reagan seemed to move past his near-death assassination attempt and get on with his life. And in praying for the other man, he probably was a happier person than he would have been.

If ever in doubt about how much emphasis you should put on things in the present and future, compared to those behind you in the past, remember the following idea every time you drive your car: Your windshield of opportunities is much bigger than the fast-receding history you happen to catch in your rear-view mirror.

If you want to be rid of moments and memories from the past, this is a good time to practice your visualization technique. Close your eyes and watch yourself put all of that mental baggage into a big bin bag, tie it up, and throw it away. You can mentally hurl the bag into space, burn it, or let it disintegrate before your eyes and let the dust blow away in the warm breeze. You don't have to lug around the past. It happened, but it doesn't have to keep happening in your future. Every time you remember it, it replays in your mind. When that happens, your mind and body feel the same as the first time it happened. This muscle memory and mental memory is not helpful for building a beautiful future. As hard as it may be, accept that it happened. Perhaps it wasn't ideal. Maybe it was horrible. It cannot be undone. However, if you focus on it, it will haunt you. You certainly don't need that extra baggage.

Let bygones be.

II. Five minutes to freak out

One of the best suggestions I've seen about how to deal with those tough times that we will all encounter in life, was in the book, *The Miracle Morning*, by Hal Elrod. He got the idea from his boss that you can give yourself five minutes to freak out and then move on. This tactic was in respect to missing out on a sale, as he worked for a sales company at the time. The idea is to give yourself five minutes to get upset, get cross, shout, tear paper, cry or whatever you do to let off steam without harming yourself or anyone else. You can even set an alarm or countdown timer on your phone. Then, when the five minutes are up, bundle up that baggage and get rid of it, not to be thought of again.

KEY POINTS

CHAPTER 4 – REGRET: WOULDA, COULDA, SHOULDA

- Words such as would have, could have, and should have usually convey a negative sentiment. Stop yourself and choose better words or phrases.

- The past is in the past. Move on and look forward to a better future. Learn from your past, but only take the lessons with you.

- Dispose of your baggage. You don't need it where you're going.

Chapter 5. Rewrite your programming

The great news is that you can rewrite your programming. That's right! Everything that you know, you have learned or thought up yourself. Whether it is spelling, how to walk, the language you speak, or how to ride a bicycle, you have learned this information or made it up. Fortunately, you can rewrite all of it. You can delete things or simply write over the old ideas with new and better ideas. You have done this loads of times too. For example, you may have learned how to get from one class to another at secondary school. Then the next year, you may have had to learn how to get to different classes. You will have also had to do this when you have moved house or changed jobs.

A few simple technics to begin rewriting your programming are as follows:

- Become more curious, especially about the opposite of what you currently think.
- Search for ideas that are new to you.
- Listen to the points of view of others and understand why they have that perspective.
- Use this greater awareness to allow yourself to have options.
- Use repetition to ingrain thoughts you find more helpful.
- Use visual clues such as Post It notes and pictures to remind you of the new ideas.

From here, in this chapter we will look more in-depth at a couple of the best ways to help you rewrite your programming — and make it stick!

I. Appreciation and gratitude

As you start to consistently achieve your daily goals, my best advice is to start appreciating the changes you are making and success you are having. Appreciate how you are progressing, the challenges you've overcome, and the effort that you've been putting in to improve your life. Too frequently we skip this step and we don't appreciate all the time, effort, and thought that we have put into learning how to improve in an area. By following the instructions you have been given in this book and by doing the exercises or tasks, you will start to get the results you wanted. You will begin to see yourself maintaining your new results and realize how great it feels to have this brilliant new habit!

Action: Take your pen or pencil and write the following in either the margin (if you don't have paper handy) or in your journal/on your notepad: Write out at least five things that you appreciate about your efforts so far. Do it right now. Remember this, *thinking* of five things means you're at step one. *Writing* five things, or more, means you're moving into step two of achievement mode. Well done!

Some options to get you started practicing appreciation and gratitude are set out below:

- I am grateful that I have good health which allows me to start walking more.
- I am grateful for the life I am leading and the endless opportunities I'm beginning to see.
- I appreciate the effort my co-workers put in every day because it makes my job easier.
- I appreciate the quiet time my family has given me to focus on this new goal.
- I have done three exercises so far today and I am proud of myself for taking these first steps.

By appreciating what you have done, you are giving feedback to yourself. This, in turn, will make you feel good about the effort you've put in and make you want to push on to start seeing additional or greater results. Things get easier to push through once you start seeing better results. Until that moment, it is worth taking just a few minutes each day to appreciate and be grateful for the time, effort, and thought you have put into getting to this point so far.

Oh, and you are best advised to continue doing the appreciation and gratefulness exercises and writing each day, even after you achieve some or all of the success you were looking for. The gratitude and appreciation exercise will become a habit itself, so it will seem easy to do later on. It might eventually even seem odd not doing them. (It does for me.)

When you stop appreciating habits, people, and things, they start to slip slowly out of your life until you wake up one day and find they are gone (it's like a country song!). This happens with money, fitness, time, spouses, children, and careers, to name but a few. This is a good time to recall the section about the pain of discipline or the pain of regret. The loss of things usually causes a lot of emotional pain which could have been avoided with a daily habit of appreciation and gratitude taking just 3-10 minutes every day — the same time it would take to use the toilet, have a snack, get a coffee, or read an article in your favorite magazine or newspaper. This is all it takes to start on a path to incredible life-changing activity. Try it!

I noticed this as one of the main contributors to my success and to the success of others I know, have observed, or have coached. Those who struggled with achieving things were often not appreciating and being grateful for the time, effort, and thought they were putting in. This, in part, is why they struggled to get the results they were looking for. They might have gotten patchy results or no results at all. In other cases, they achieved some results but they didn't appreciate the results, were unhappy, didn't wish to continue, or they would slip back and lose some ground. This could be attributed to them not having reflected on, and truly appreciated, what it took to get there from their own efforts.

One of the key things that appreciation and gratitude do is focus your attention on what you have and each of the many steps you have achieved. This creates a positive feedback loop which encourages you to do more and get that good feeling again. So, add these tools of appreciation and gratitude to your toolkit and use them every day.

For more information on appreciation go to www.scottsbook.com/achieveanything/appreciation

II. Visualize

Finding the new you:

Strange as this might sound, sometimes it's easier to find the new you in someone else. Let me explain. If you want to lose weight and be a certain size, then who can you think of who you would end up looking similar to when your transformation has finished? Who has similar characteristics or physical attributes/proportions to you that you would like when your project is done? Now you may already know who it is and that would be great. I will get to what you do next, in a few paragraphs, if that is the case. However, if that is not the case, you need to spend a little bit of time thinking about it, and then finding someone who you could make your avatar or destination person. This helps greatly in tandem with the visualization process.

The real you!

So the idea is two-fold. First of all, you want to find, in your mind, a picture of what you will look like when you are finished losing weight, getting more toned, or getting fit. You need to be able to see the end result in your mind. You need to train your mind to think about what you are going to look like when you are done this transformation. You also need to accept that this is the new you. Then, by constantly repeating this visualization of the new you, your brain will automatically begin to act as if it is already there, at the destination. (More on this, act-as-if, leverage tool in chapter 13). So if you want to be thinner, your mind will start to have you do things such as being mindful of what you eat, how much you eat, when you eat, and how you eat. It will also start having you think about your physical activity and exercise; when you are doing it, how you are doing it, where you do it and how frequently you do it.

> *"We all act consistently with our view of who we truly are, whether that view is accurate or not."*
>
> **–Tony Robbins**

Consistency with our own self-image is a very significant determinant in succeeding with any of our goals in life. You tend to act in line with your self-image. If you start acting outside of the image you hold for yourself, you will feel quite uncomfortable. This feeling will continue until you allow your brain to make the shift to the new you or until you snap back and return to acting like you expected yourself to.

If you see yourself as shy, you will act shy, by your definition, because that is the way you believe you are. If you start acting more assertively, confident, and outgoing, it will feel very odd. You may even feel fake. You will then need to continue with this exposure therapy of trying out a new characteristic until you gradually become more comfortable with it. Then, as you see yourself doing it, you can shift your self-image to accept that you are sometimes more outgoing than you were or than others are. Each day you act and shift your mindset to believe the changes you see, the closer you will get to adjusting your self- image and your actions. Continue on this road to build an unstoppable characteristic.

Alternatively, as you try behaving differently than the self-image you hold of yourself, you may snap back to your old ways as an instinctive reaction to being inconsistent with your self-image. Being inconsistent with your self-image must either be endured and encouraged, as you act to gradually change it, or you must revert to your old ways. Your physical manifestation must follow and be consistent with the image and thoughts you hold of yourself.

Your mind is like a heat-seeking missile. Once it is clear on the exact coordinates, metrics, or details of the target you are seeking, it locks onto those coordinates and goes straight for it. Therefore, the more precise you can make the coordinates or metrics, the more accurate your results will be. If you're not precise with the coordinates or metrics that you want to lock onto, your mind moves from being a heat-seeking missile of modern times, to more of a cannon from the 1600s. It is useful to make a mess of the general area, but rarely lands directly on target to nail the result desired. Vague goals will deliver vague results.

For example, saying you want to lose a few pounds isn't very helpful. Directionally it is good. But to get a specific result, you need to lock onto a specific target. If you are trying to lose 20 pounds, from 180 down to 160, from March to June, you could write the following: "I weigh 160 pounds as of today, the 10th June." This makes it specific, affirmed in the present tense, and time bound in the future. This is something your mind can lock onto and you will know if you have hit the target on the date. By affirming your goal in the present, you will also be reinforcing your new you each time you repeat or affirm your goal. In addition, as you think of yourself as slimmer and fitter, you are more likely to start acting in accordance with your new persona. Slimmer people tend to eat fewer calories and fitter people tend to eat better calories and are more active.

So, not only would it be good to have a clear and precise vision of what you would look like sporting your new metrics, it also can be helpful to have an external avatar body double. This image of what you would like to look like will help your mind to believe it is possible that your body can be the size that you are aiming to be. This is especially true in the early days of trying to shift from one characteristic to another. Do a search on the internet, or find your favorite magazine, and flip through and start finding people that you would look similar to if you had the body shape that you are after. Look for someone who is the same or similar height, age, hair, skin tone, etc. The closer they are to looking like you, the more likely your mind will accept that it is possible for you to look the same.

I already know my avatar

If you already know who it is and the picture you want of that person, simply get it from the magazine or the internet and cut it out or print it off to put it on your wall. Put it in a place where you will see it at least twice a day and ideally more. You could tape it to your mirror and fridge, as well as paste it into your day-timer and workbook at the back page. Then, every day you can look at it, throughout the day, and remind yourself of the target shape you're aiming to have. This sometimes helps more than just visualizing your own body in a new shape, because the other one may be more believable to you and you can imagine what they would do to keep that body in that shape. You can even read about how people keep their body in the condition they have by reading up on their eating and exercise habits.

To this end, and as you'll read more about later, I stumbled upon Daniel Craig, who played 007 in several of the James Bond movies. I used a picture of him to remind me, on a daily basis, what my target was. I found this worked very well for me because he is the same height as me and he had the waist size I was targeting and that I once had. So I could see proportionately how his body was built and what mine would look like if I accomplished similar metrics. As you get closer to your goal, you can see how your body has been evolving and adjust accordingly, unless you want to look exactly the same as a movie star or global celebrity!

This exercise works equally well for all kinds of goals. Pick a particular sporting hero, if you want to be a better golfer or tennis player, or an award-winning writer or entertainer. Just make sure the picture is of them winning a tournament, performing a fantastic backswing, winning an Academy Award or doing whatever it is they do best that you are trying to copy. This mental association with their success will further inspire and motivate you to reach your goal sooner.

If you don't know who your avatar could be, ask friends which body they think would look good as a proxy for you and where you want to be. Find out what metrics they have that you would like to emulate. It's quite simple to do in today's world. Find a favorite actor or person online and search for their measurements (waist, weight, height, etc.). Put a great picture of them on your fridge. My sister-in-law's partner did this when he wanted to slim down and tone up.

Decide you will have the same body measurements as they do by a specific date. Then work backwards from that date to today and calculate what weekly targets you will need to meet. Then assess what you will need to do on a daily basis to reach those weekly targets. Finally, re-affirm your commitment, review your purpose for doing this, and, if your Why is strong enough, you will succeed in achieving your goal.

KEY POINTS

CHAPTER 5 – REWRITE YOUR PROGRAMMING

> You CAN rewrite your programming!

> Use repetition, visual clues and other techniques to improve your programming

> By appreciating what you have done, you are giving feedback to yourself. Things get easier to push through once you start seeing better results. Until that moment, it is worth taking just a few minutes each day to appreciate and be grateful for the time, effort, and thought you have put into getting to this point so far.

> Appreciation and gratitude create a positive feedback loop to further encourage you.

> Find the 'new you' traits in someone else to help you progress towards that ideal you.

> You tend to act in line with the self-image you currently hold.

> Your mind is like a heat-seeking missile. Once it is clear on the exact coordinates, metrics, or details of the target you are seeking, it locks onto those coordinates and goes straight for it.

> Vague goals attract vague results but precision in planning improves probable results.

> Decide on your Avatar.

> If your Why is strong enough, you will succeed in achieving your goal.

STEP 2

ACTIONS... TO HELP YOU *OVERCOME*

‣ Consider your beliefs and why you have those particular beliefs.

‣ Identify the challenges you need to overcome.

‣ Challenge any beliefs you have that make you uncomfortable.

‣ Take a few moments to perform the reflect, rehearse and visualize exercise about a situation that might make you uncomfortable or anxious. (see page 40)

‣ Question yourself. Are your beliefs about money allowing you maximum joy?

‣ Sometimes we think we will feel great when we achieve something, and we don't. Challenge your Why and keep moving forward.

‣ Confront the brutal reality about your beliefs and decide which ones to keep or leave behind. Write down your beliefs and assess them.

‣ Adopt strategies to get past your beliefs – the three-step process. (see page 47)

  • Remove limiting beliefs.

  • Detour around limiting beliefs.

  • Change limiting beliefs.

‣ Practice using more empowering, future-oriented phrases.

‣ Use the visualization technique to help you be rid of moments and memories from the past.

> Use the five minutes to freak out strategy to deal with those tough times we will all encounter in life.

> Use a few simple technics to begin rewriting your programme.

> Continue doing the appreciation and gratefulness exercises and writing each day, even after you achieve some or all of the success you were looking for. For more information on appreciation go to www.scottsbook.com/achieveanything/appreciation

> Find the new you. Use visualization and exposure techniques.

> Put a picture of your goal in prominent places in your house.

INTERMISSION

Congratulations!!!

You are about a third of the way through the book, and I am sure your mind is abuzz with new ideas and a desire to start working on them.

Continue to use this book like a workbook by underlining key passages, making notes in the margins, and highlighting items you would like to return to.

Why not book 30 minutes in your diary right now, for later this week. It will be the time that you can start doing more of the activities you've read about in this book.

These concepts are not just to be understood with a nod and knowing feeling of, "I know" or "I'll do it later." They must be acted upon and completed! To save you from some disappointment and having to read three more books similar to this, you must make this a workbook and take action as prescribed.

The intent of this book is to help you create growing success in your life, not merely be an academic and interesting leisure read. In the end, you have to do your own pushups. I can describe better technique, but you will need to put the time in your diary, daily, and take the actions you clearly outlined, daily, to increase the probability that you will get the results you are looking for.

Now let's get back to becoming unstoppable!

STEP 3 - **WRITE**

The purpose of this section is to have you commit your thoughts to paper. The saying that, "The pen is mightier than the sword," is indicative of how powerful the written word is. Writing down thoughts will help to keep things straight in your mind and should stop you from going around in circles or covering the same ground numerous times.

Writing also helps you paint a clear picture that you can pick up and revisit with clarity whenever you want. Important things are in written form, such as tickets, contracts, love letters, and exams. So, given the high importance of your life and your future, it stands to reason that you should write down some things on your road to achieve anything.

If you don't already have a few things written down, this would be a good time to do so. From Step 1 — Think, you could have a few notes written about where you want to be one day. You might also have noted down some of the mindset challenges you have which could be holding you back and would be helpful to address, as noted in Step 2 — Overcome.

Now you can get a little creative. This may make you excited with the endless possibilities. However, if you feel at all uncomfortable, stick with it. Like exposure therapy, you are getting familiar with what is unfamiliar to you. Stay with it as you learn to make it more familiar and you will get more comfortable with the topic the more you work through it.

Chapter 6. The Imagination Game

What is the most exciting and wonderful thing you can think of doing in your future? Is it building an exciting career, taking an exotic foreign holiday, winning in a favorite sporting event, developing a deep relationship, or perhaps obtaining a diploma or degree? Open your mind to all those dreams you had as a 6-, 10- or 18-year-old. Get revved up and interested in this next chapter of your life. Take a few minutes and let your mind wander through the universe of potential right now. Consider the exciting possibilities that you would love in your life. Take a minute and dream a little.

Welcome back.

I. Imagination: Use it or lose it

To capture this great stuff, once again grab a pen and some paper or a device like a phone, tablet, or laptop. Write on the paper or into the device or even use the speech technology and dictate your thoughts now. If it helps, get yourself somewhere you can feel open and free and imaginative (your bedroom, 5-star hotel lobby, back garden, etc.). This is your time to get creative with untethered possibilities! Spend a few minutes on this and at least get a few draft ideas down in writing before you move to the next section.

You may be able to do this right now. Though I'll understand if you need a few runs at this across a few days.

As I mentioned, you may be out of training. You might feel silly or uncomfortable wanting new adventures and other great things in your life. No worries. Stick with the process and press on through the feelings and continue writing. Practice. Train your brain. You are allowed to dream and make those dreams come true.

Others of you may have pent up desires come pouring out in a gushing tidal wave of excitement and opportunity. Write bullet points and capture as much as you can. You can come back to those points and build on them in a few minutes or in a day or two.

If you want to prime the pump a little, then here are a few ways to reimagine your future.

- Think back to what you enjoyed doing in your teens. Was it creating or listening to music, playing a particular sport, writing creative stories, researching facts, traveling to different locations, or maybe creating art or acting? What were you enjoying or dreaming about back then? Who were your idols? What were your ambitions?
- Consider what magazines you buy. Think about the daily, weekly, or monthlies but also the one-off and special ones you buy on rare occasions. These will give you some insight into what you like seeing, doing, reading, and being involved in.
- Take a trip down memory lane. You may even want to flip through some of your favorite holiday snaps or other photos. What you are looking for is those 'ah yes' moments where you remember feeling so alive and vibrant and powerful. Whatever you were doing in those moments will help you understand yourself more and guide you towards your dreams.

So, put down the book for three minutes (set a timer) and write down some ideas that make you smile and outline a future you'll look forward to.

II. Assessing and sorting

It's very exciting to have some of those old dreams dusted off and written down. Hopefully, you are feeling like they are just a tiny bit more real now and some may actually happen. Relax about the ones where you're not sure whether you want to do them anymore or think you could no longer do them. Just park those and relax. Focus on the others for the moment.

With what you have written down in the exercise above, next to each of your creative ideas, note a time period for completion such as now, in six months, or five years from now. Also note down those items that you believe are possible now and those more likely to be done later. Finally, write down next to each item, which ones you are really passionate about and which are simply nice-to-haves.

This separation method helps take the pressure off of having too many ideas, dreams, or goals competing for your time, resources, and head space. Now you will start to have a picture of the priorities you will have.

Now that you have some ideas that you are passionate about and would like to do straight away, you are on the road to achievement. You will be able to narrow your final few ideas down to one or two, maximum. I believe it is very hard to succeed at more than three things during any period of time in life. These are usually your primary income source, a relationship or family and one other item — your new activity or dream goal.

III. Break out — Your get out of jail free card

Sometimes people struggle with this part a little bit. This is partly due to aging. As you get older than 25, you harden the walls of your self-imposed mental prison. The barriers, limits, and challenges you see are your own mind's creation. Your perception of your personal circumstances is what has you trapped, not the reality that exists.

Feeling a little poetic at this point, I've noted down a brief poem about how habits can creep up on you with detrimental effects.

> Thought habits that you got comfortable with,
>
> When they were flimsy like a spider's web,
>
> Could imprison you if left unchallenged
>
> Swirling in your head.

Along that theme, there have been many variations in history. One that is similar comes from the Sage of Omaha, which I have written out for you below.

> *"The chains of habit are too light to be felt until they are too heavy to be broken."*
>
> **Warren Buffett**

Like an old bolt on a screw, it might be tight, or have rust on it, making it harder to turn. So it can be difficult to get it turning at the start. But you need to stick with it or get some help— maybe some WD40 in this case. Maybe the third or fourth time you try to turn it, it will have loosened enough that it gets moving. Then it does usually get easier to remove the bolt from that point.

Using your imagination can feel the same way. A little tough to start, but will get easier with effort and persistence. Consider these pointers below like the WD40 that gets things lubricated.

For those of you who would like some extra help to turn on the tap of imagination, you can try the following suggestions:

- Do not judge what you write. Just let it be an option on the table of life.
- Let your spirit soar and channel your inner superstar. Let yourself have these dreams on paper. It doesn't matter where you are now or the circumstances in which you find yourself currently. Press on!
- Think of someone who has done it already — a friend, a famous person, or another person you know. Knowing that something has been done before can inspire us.
- Put the effort in. Work on using your imagination every day for 5 minutes. Book an appointment with yourself in your diary and keep to it. It's like a muscle that needs to be built up and used. Use it or lose it as they say.

KEY POINTS

CHAPTER 6 – THE IMAGINATION GAME

- ‣ Write things down!
- ‣ Writing down thoughts will help to keep things straight in your mind and should stop you from going around in circles or covering the same ground numerous times.
- ‣ Having some ideas that you are passionate about and would like to do straight away, puts you on the road to achievement.
- ‣ The barriers, limits and challenges you see are your own mind's creation.
- ‣ Using your imagination can feel a little tough to start, but will get easier with effort and persistence.

Chapter 7. Decide what you want (and write it down)

I assume you are reading this because you want to change at least one thing in your life. You might not realize this, but you may have to change several things in your life to get one significant thing changed. "What!!" you howl. I just want to lose weight, stop smoking, be on time, make more money, get fit, run a marathon, be a better mum/dad.... The list goes on. Maybe you want all of these. Or more! Or just some of these things (to start!). Maybe you want them all, but you have your prioritization list and will want to get one significant goal done first.

Momentum

What we saw in the previous chapter was that, if you get one goal done, you gain momentum. This momentum, in turn, will make it easier to get your second, third, and fourth goal done. The first goal that you achieve will have helped or strengthened some habits that are now ingrained in you. You will accomplish new things, both thoughts and actions, which you won't even have to think about anymore. These new things will automatically occur because of their now deep habitual nature. Your new habit(s) will give you strength without reducing focus; like breathing or walking. This will free your mind to work on your second, third, and then fourth goals. Helpfully though, because of your earlier success, you will go forward with added momentum, a fresh new feel-good factor, as well as with enhanced personal strength and increased confidence! Ta da!

Improve with goals

We all want to improve ourselves in some way. And by improve, I mean it could be a small improvement or a large improvement: it could just be putting the toothpaste top back on the toothpaste tube every morning and night. Or the improvement you want could be as large as creating a passive income of $1 million a month, for the Rest. Of. Your. Life. Nice! It could be a financial goal, physical goal, spiritual goal, or a family/relationship goal. Whatever your highest priority goal is, let's focus on that for the moment.

The Law of Unintended Consequences (LUC)

This is when you take purposeful action and one or more outcomes from that action were not intended or foreseen. One thing always seems to impact many other things and this Law recognizes that idea. It reminds us to be mindful that many things, both inside and outside of our awareness, will be impacted in some way by our actions. These can be both good things and less good things.

Earlier, I said you would probably have to change a number of things, even though you may only want to change one significant thing. What I meant by that was that it's hard to improve in one area in isolation. We usually see the Law of Unintended Consequences come into play here. Let's take the example of quitting smoking. Quitting smoking probably would be easier if you did not spend any time with other smokers and you spent more time with fresh air folks or freshers.

As an aside, currently I am using "fresh air folks" or "freshers" as the definition of someone who does not smoke. I prefer to use these terms rather than using the non-smoking/smoke-free/non-smoker tags. It seems odd to define ourselves by what we aren't or don't do. It would seem strange for adults to refer to themselves as non-alien, non-monkey or beyond-baby. I believe it is better for us to focus our mind on the thing we are or want to be and no longer remind ourselves of the thing we don't want or are moving away from — in this case smoke/smoking.

Not spending time with other smokers would mean you would be less likely to see, smell, or discuss smoking and thereby greatly remove the temptation to smoke based on your environmental cues. You would be less likely to be offered a cigarette or be tempted to smoke and less likely to be reminded about the perceived joys of smoking or why you smoked. In addition, it probably would be easier to quit smoking if you didn't buy cigarettes. To stop buying cigarettes, it would be easier if you did not go to the shop where you had the habit of buying cigarettes. The reason for this is that when you go into that shop, you may be triggered, mentally and physically (muscle memory), into the habits that you had around buying cigarettes when you were in that shop. Think of the things you would habitually do like approach the counter, point to the pack, or nod to the cashier. Sometimes the cashier knows you so well they already have your packs down from the shelf, on the counter, and rung into the till while you are still five steps away. Lovely, unless you are trying to quit.

It might also be easier if you didn't go to the places where you used to smoke. That could mean in your car, in your house, at a friend's house, outside your office, on a walk, etc. Fortunately for people trying to quit smoking today, there are far fewer places where you can actually smoke. This has undoubtedly helped people to stop smoking, or reduce the amount they smoke, because there are far fewer places where smoking is permitted.

It would also be useful when trying to stop smoking to give up activities that you would do when you were smoking. This could be something like reading a certain magazine, watching tv or a movie, or even meeting up with a friend for a drink in the local bar, pub or cafe.

If achieving a fresher lifestyle is not on your goal list because you already have a fresh air lifestyle, or you still haven't been convinced by the benefits of one, then think of what your priority goal is and substitute that into the fresh air example I outlined above. Think through how you can set up your environment to help you achieve your goal.

So you can see there are a number of actions that would help you quit smoking, or achieve any other goal, if you adjusted some other decisions as well. Most of the items to change will be trigger or support functions. Another hard part about giving up smoking would be not shopping in places you used to shop, which may be very convenient for you but not helpful while you're trying to quit smoking. Of course you can shop there again later once you are re-trained/re-programmed, are confident with your new habits, and have the personal strength not to be triggered. By reducing or replacing several or all of these triggers and supports, you will increase your chance of early success dramatically!

Changes in your environment – *reduce or replace*

You may not want to completely cut off some friends, but you may wish to reduce the amount of time you spend with certain friends or associates. This is especially true for those friends who are smokers and extra-especially those friends who are encouraging you to continue to be a smoker. So you can reduce the amount of time spent with certain friends from say five hours per week down to maybe 2 hours per week. You could reduce the number of times you visit the shop where you buy your cigarettes (*used to* buy your cigarettes) from two visits a week down to one visit a week, or even better, zero visits per week.

Also, you could replace or reduce the activities that you used to do while smoking. While reducing the other activities, you could replace them with some more positive or healthy activities. For example, instead of driving to your friend's house to sit in front of the tv and watch some shows while smoking cigarettes, you could walk to another friend's house and go for a walk together for 20 minutes or half an hour. This is the same length of time as one tv show, but arguably better for you. You would have the benefits of a healthy walk outdoors and building a better relationship with your friend through chatting.

You would not be smoking, nor sitting, nor watching a show someone created to keep your attention. The show would also keep you away from attaining some goals that might really make you feel like a superstar and maybe even turn you into one. This must be better than watching some other superstar on tv living your life! This slight change in your activity would create the added benefit of spending more time with a new, positive, fresh air friend. It would also help you develop a new habit of walking, which has several very helpful health benefits, which may also encourage a fresh air lifestyle.

So you can see, in wanting to change one key thing (i.e. smoking), it may be helpful to change several things in your life (i.e. habits, fitness, relationships, hangouts). This can reduce triggers and lead to better support mechanisms and social circles, which can improve your situation and increase your probability of success. Of course, if you don't make the other changes, they may happen anyway due to the Law of Unintended Consequences.

This example highlights becoming smoke free and remaining a fresh air advocate for life but the steps, ideas, and the critical factor of making changes to your environment can be used when trying to achieve anything.

Don't need to change

Now, you don't *have* to change your friends, your shopping habits, or all your activities. I am simply pointing out that, if you did make these other small changes, they may help you more quickly achieve your bigger goal. Moreover, as a consequence of achieving your main goal, you may find that some of your old habits and activities will simply change on their own anyway.

Other unintended consequences

In fact, you may find that some of your smoking friends will naturally choose to spend less time with you because you have become a non-smoker. You would no longer be in their tribe. You see, they may find it difficult spending time with a non-smoker, especially seeing you achieve your goals while they may not be achieving theirs. Or they may feel that you are not quite your old self anymore and they may not feel that the relationship is as strong as it once was. Some people even feel they have been left behind or you have turned your back on them. They will even jokingly say things like, "Oh, they have gone over to the other side or the Dark Side." Some smokers simply enjoy the activity so much that they have no interest in quitting and enjoy being around other smokers more.

Benefits

A friend of ours, who has smoked for over 15 years and is a digital marketing superstar, recalls the exact moment he knew he had to finally quit smoking. He was at Alan Carr's Easy Way to Stop Smoking seminar and the speaker noted that the cigarette industry spent billions every year on marketing and promotion. The speaker reminded the crowd that these tobacco companies employed hundreds of top-flight marketing people, both in-house and through agencies, to ensure that their brand was seen and purchased. Of course, what is marketing without showcasing all the benefits of the product in question, he continued. So he asked the assembled crowd to take out their cigarette packages and look at them for the list of benefits. Despite billions spent on influencing campaigns, packaging, and countless gurus in marketing, they decided not to list any of the benefits on the packaging. The penny dropped. There were no benefits. That was the last day he smoked. That was many years ago.

Looking forward

As you make these changes in your life, it is best to look forward to the life you want to have. This may mean spending time with people you don't even know yet. Now that may make some of you a little uncomfortable. However, isn't that the way you met all the friends you have now? At one point in time, they were people you did not know. Whether you feel you need to change some friends or not, undoubtedly it is important to surround yourself with people who make your life more joyful.

Changing people in your life

It was Joshua and Ryan from The Minimalist Podcast who I first heard say the following phrase, "You can't change the people in your life, but you can change the people in your life." This is a brilliant saying. Read it again. If the people around you will not change for the better (better for them and you), then it may be time to start spending less time with them and more time with other, more supportive people.

The five people you spend the most time with

This concept is so very important, particularly when you consider Jim Rohn's famous saying, "You are the average of the five people you spend the most time with." This is an excellent observation and is so useful to recognize its importance in your own life. You probably spend the most time with people who earn a similar amount of money as you do. And if you are active, you are likely to spend the most time with people of a similar caliber of athleticism (note your league level, speed, distance, etc.).

If you want to improve your skills in football, find people better at football than you and spend more time with them. When you want to read more books and talk to people about books, join a book club or a library group. When you want to make more money in your life, start spending more time with people who make more money than you. Find people you can learn from and allocate ever-increasing amounts of time with them. You will improve in many different ways, not just in the one you set out to improve.

Personal strength

There is one other thing you will notice as you start to take control of your life and make the changes that you need to make in order to start living the life of your dreams. This one other thing is your own personal strength. You will need some extra strength to help you grow because there will be challenges on this new path, as there are on any path, even the one you are currently on. There will be resistance, naysayers, and people who don't want you to improve your life. There will be people who say you should stay as you are and there will be those who will fight against your changes because of what they want, not because of what you want.

It will require all of your strength to face the challenges head-on and continue down the path that you have chosen for yourself. That will take inner strength. And you have that inner strength. It may just be a muscle that you haven't used for a while or isn't as strong as you would like it to be yet. Not to worry though! Your mental strength will grow over the weeks and months and things will get easier as you practice using it. See how good it feels to take control of your situation and continue to press forward, step-by-step, day-by-day, as you continue to get closer to your goal and develop new supportive and powerful habits.

Horse to water: Let it go!

Let go of the concern that you can't take these people with you on your journey. You may want them with you, but they may not want to come or be able to commit to the journey. Let them continue on their path and when they're ready, they will, or won't, move on too. As the saying goes, "You can lead a horse to water, but you can't make it drink." Remember, this is *your* goal and *your* new path, so ignore everyone else and focus on taking the next steps for you.

For some quick start help or more information about how to get started, go to www.scottsbook.com/achieveanything/startnow.

I. Select the best Imagination Game ideas; Sifting while shifting

Now that you've had a few minutes to let those initial dreams and ideas percolate in your mind, it's time to review them. If you are absolutely clear on the goal you would like to pursue next, skip down to part II below. Otherwise, continue reading here.

It's time to once again, grab that pen and paper or device and start making some notes. While fresh in your mind, jot down the key elements that excite or intrigue you most about your favorite five ideas. Don't spend time on more than five though. More than that and your energy and ability to deliver will reduce and you may not succeed with any of them. Remember, once you have something going reasonably well with habits, systems, knowledge, and some success, then you can add another option into your life.

Like an airplane, it takes incredible energy and focus to get it off the ground and above the clouds. However, once you are cruising at 33,000 feet, you can focus on the next thing.

Remember, you are the author of your life. Describe the life you see for yourself. Write it down. It will start to unfold for you as you take conscious and unconscious steps toward the outcomes you've noted.

II. Understand your Why for going after the goal

A. How to find your why (Ask why? Why? Why?) (see example coming up).
B. What calls to you, your passions (what do you read, watch, discuss, collect, think about).
C. What is your Why now, but also write down what your Why was at 6-, 10-, 15- and 20-years-old. This will be instructive.
D. Write down your motivations for your Why.
E. Write what makes you excited and nervous/anxious about this Why.
F. How to move past any anxiety.

"If you know the why you can live any how."

–Frederick Nietzsche

Deep purpose

Your purpose. Your Why. Your, "what is the point of all this?" This is the most valuable piece of information about yourself, at this time, that you could have. You see, when you have an understanding and clarity about why you want to be, do, have, or achieve something, then you can get those powerful emotions and determination behind your drive. Your purpose will continue to motivate you, inspire you, and push you through all of the difficult challenges that there will be on the road to successfully achieving each thing that you want in life.

How do you find your Why? My best advice would be to sit down with a pen and paper and write down why you want to do the thing you're thinking about. Then, underneath your answer, write the question Why? Then think about why you want that situation or result. Then repeat this exercise straight away by writing the question Why? Underneath your previous answer and answer it again.

Here is an example using income

I believe many of you will have thought about increasing your income. You may have even wondered how you could make this income in a more passive way. As most people are familiar with money, I will use an income example to highlight this tactic below:

Start with an initial statement of what you want and say it as precisely as you can. For example:

I would like to have a consistent, monthly, after-tax, passive income of $25,000. Or more. By the 16th of March 2030.

Why?

Because it would be great to have a good income without having to spend my day working at a job I dislike. And I believe that $25,000, or more, would be significant enough to meet all of my basic needs and most of my wishes too from 2030 and beyond.

Why?

Because I would like the freedom to choose what I do with my days. In addition, I believe $25,000+ per month would give me confidence and calm knowing that my bills are easily taken care of every month.

Why?

For freedom: I would like freedom of time so I can enjoy my time with my family and friends and have time for my own exploration, relaxation, and meaningful projects.

For $25,000+: By knowing I have a significant income coming in monthly, I can take my mind off the money part of life, be more relaxed, and truly enjoy those things in my life that I have focused on — my time freedom.

Why?

Because some of my highest values are family and freedom. It's a blessing to be able to enjoy time with my family and do work I love, when I want, and with people I want to spend my time with.

Take this highest value, for this project, to be your driving vision for your life, at this time, until you write down a different one. This is now the number one purpose for all things that you do. So, any time somebody suggests something to do or a way to spend your time, you need to filter it through this purpose statement, this "why?" statement. If anything doesn't quite fit into this, then you need to adjust what you are doing or going to do. This may mean saying no to things that seem interesting, fun, or fascinating, but are not compelling or supportive of this driving vision, or Why. At least you are being clear and decisive at this stage in your life.

When is the best time to figure out where you should be going? The best time is before you need to and as early in life as you can. Certainly, you want to do it before you start thinking about where you have gotten to. Ideally you consider and plan the future you want before you get to that point where so much has gone wrong or not gone to plan. Too many times we wait until something really significant happens in life (too frequently it's a setback or a challenge) and we find we have to change a "should" to a "must."

You may have wanted to lose weight. Maybe you wanted to be slimmer or fitter for years. Yet it was always too far down the priority list in the "should" section to be tackled when you found some time. But then the doctor tells you that you have early-onset diabetes, heart disease, or some other weight, health or fitness challenge and it needs to be addressed immediately. It is often only at this moment that we finally decide to turn our want or "should" into a "must" and take action on these things. Don't wait! Start right now.

III. Go bigger

Whatever ideas you have now for your future, try to think bigger and expand the realm of possibilities. Add a more exciting element to your goals. Set goals that, when you write them down, make you feel a little uneasy, either about whether you could achieve them or what other people might think about your goal. Being uneasy, or uncomfortable, around some of your bigger goals means you are stretching beyond what you already know you can do. And that's perfectly fine and as it should be. Besides, you are probably already feeling a little uncomfortable with where you are in life. And that uncomfortable feeling usually gets worse with inaction and across time. Whereas, being uncomfortable for a short while, as you improve in a new space, is short-lived. And you will soon be feeling much better as you shift from uncomfortable to unstoppable!

"You're 100% satisfied with your life exactly the way it is because otherwise it'd be different."

–Larry Winget

The President doesn't get training or experience as the President before they become the President. The CEO doesn't get experience as CEO until they become the CEO. But they need to know that, if they want to do it, they will need to be a little uncomfortable. That is the same for you in anything that you do. You will need to feel uncomfortable, uneasy, uncertain. You will need to start to consider how you can achieve the bigger goal. You will need to do things that you haven't done, think things you haven't thought and be the you that you haven't been yet. There can be a lot of resistance around this idea. Fear often creeps in and excuses, stories, and reasons can start to emerge. But you've got that covered because you are learning how to deal with, and overcome these issues, from this book.

One of the trickier excuses or reasons for not wanting to achieve a goal is because the person "just wants to be me." If this is you, what you mean is you want to be the me you are right now which isn't even the me you were three years ago (because we are constantly changing whether we notice or not). But you trick yourself into believing it is better to be the me you are now rather than the me you will be when you achieve your goals (or the me you will be if you don't achieve your goals — either way you are always changing in form and thought).

Your reasoning may save you a lot of time and will stop you from having to think differently, learn, apply, or achieve things. However, you will also not become someone better or different. And why wouldn't you want that? Especially if it is simply a better version of you! Perhaps a happier version of you because you've achieved your goals. So, don't let the reasons win. Go for the results! In time you will see that you really can achieve anything.

KEY POINTS

CHAPTER 7 – DECIDE WHAT YOU WANT (AND WRITE IT DOWN)

> If you write it down you can track it, check it off and then celebrate. This builds mental momentum.

> The Law of Unintended Consequences (LUC) can also come into play – This is when you take purposeful action and one or more outcomes from that action were not intended or foreseen.

> It is hard to improve in only one area in isolation.

> Focus your mind on what you want to move toward, not away from.

> By reducing or replacing several or all of the triggers and supports (around a habit you want to change), you will increase your chance of early success dramatically!

> Change your environment. Set it up for success! The people, space and places in your life need to be re-considered.

- Find people you can learn from and allocate ever-increasing amounts of time with them.

- Personal strength is key as you face challenges head-on and continue down the path that you have chosen for yourself.

- Remember, this is your goal and your new path, so ignore everyone else and focus on taking the next steps for you.

- You are the author of your life. Describe, in writing, the life you see for yourself.

- Your purpose. Your Why. Your, "what is the point of all this?" This is the most valuable piece of information about yourself, at this time, that you could have.

- You will need to do things that you haven't done, think things you haven't thought and be the you that you haven't been yet.

Chapter 8. Set Goals

One of the most important things you will do in your life is to set goals. They will guide you, inspire you, support you, and keep you focused. You will set many goals in your life — over a million — and you will achieve many of those. The secret will be to set and achieve the more significant ones while enjoying your success with the everyday variety too.

We have spoken a lot about goals in this book so far. I took the general view that if you were reading this book, you would be familiar with goals in their broader context. However, I believe this is an ideal place to go through a quick refresher on the topic of goals. In addition, we will go deeper and be more precise in our understanding of goals.

This is the ideal moment because we are finishing the step about writing things down and we are about to start planning. Writing things down usually makes us become more precise in our thoughts and the specific words we use. In combination with this, when we plan, we are best to be precise with what we are doing. As we saw in chapter one, life is as simple as planning a holiday. However, we wouldn't want to look forward to a sunshine and beach holiday and then find that our imprecision has placed us standing at the bottom of a ski slope while wearing flippers and holding a snorkel in our hands.

I. What is a goal?

By most dictionary definitions, a goal is simply an aim. It is the outcome or achievement toward which effort is directed.

Whenever you are working toward an outcome you desire or require, you are working on your goal. These outcomes can be in any area and are usually expressed as being quite simple.

Something with a lot of complex steps, like getting a person on the moon, can still be boiled down to the simple goal of putting a person on the moon.

Of course there are likely to be many, many individual steps, milestones, or mini goals that need to occur to make this broad goal happen. This is why we need a bridge between writing and planning. You can write the goal of putting a person on the moon rather quickly. However, writing out the detailed plan and all the material components will take more time, patience, and perseverance.

Chunking

Writing out the detailed steps is a process called chunking. You take a small chunk of what needs to be done and you focus on that until that item is completed. Then you move on to the next chunk that needs to be accomplished. As you accomplish more chunks, or mini goals, you move closer to completing the overall goal. The great thing about the chunking method is that it breaks larger goals down into more manageable and discreet component parts. This helps us get our mind around the next objective and makes each objective clearer.

Often, we will delay or freeze up if the next step in the process is not clear. Sometimes this happens because the goal, or a smaller chunk, is still too big or has too many competing components to it. Let's go back to the moon landing example. A person might feel that this goal is too large or challenging. The way to reframe that perspective is to look at it as a journey of 1,000 steps. You simply need to take the first step first. So, in your plan, you may have noted down that you need to, "set a budget." This may still be too large of a chunk for most people to get their head around. Therefore, you can break it up into many parts such as, "search internet for approximate cost of a rocket" and "call NASA to understand cost of fuel for the launch." Alternatively, you could search for and hire an accountant who has worked on space missions before. That person may solve all of your smaller chunking questions around budgeting.

It is useful to chunk things down to make them more manageable, but be careful not to get silly and chunk them down too much. You don't need to get so detailed that your next few steps are lift left arm, pick up telephone, dial the number for NASA and wait on the line until they respond. Try to chunk things down into their smallest discrete task without going microscopic on the tasks.

II. Why have goals?

Goals are a key part of life. They are essential to survival. Though they are also useful beyond that for achievement, self-actualization, and organizing. The basic goals of finding water, food, and shelter are critical. Imagine if you did not have access to food for a few days. Your mind, which is a target-seeking machine, will lock onto this objective of finding food and begin to use every option it can imagine to find sustenance. So you can see, goals are already part of our social structure. Once you achieve the lower-order goals, many people progress on to higher-level goals. For anyone who is aware of Maslow's Hierarchy of Needs, you will already know how we continue to set different goals throughout our lives to move through different situations in our life.

Goals can be fun, such as wanting an ice cream or going to the cinema. They can help us learn when we focus on achieving a certain score on a test or exam. The goal will motivate us to study and revise so that we can achieve the maximum performance. Goals can act as a compass on the way to another destination where we are not clear on the final outcome. This can aid discovery and help us through challenging moments in our journey.

Finally, goals can help us feel excited and alive while their achievement can fill us with confidence. When you complete a task or a goal, it feels good. We feel proud for having pushed past challenges and achieved a challenging objective. Often, the more challenging it is, the prouder we feel and the more confidence we gain for the next task at hand. Success breeds success. The more you accomplish, the more you will want to accomplish.

III. You already have goals

You may have guessed this by now, but you already have goals. And you are succeeding with many of them. You should recognize your little goals as well as your larger goals. If you only recognized and celebrated the one time you walked on the Moon, then the rest of your life would feel pretty empty and uneventful. So it is highly recommended that you acknowledge your daily successes and celebrate the smaller wins so you build confidence from these achievements. This will also help to remind you that you are more successful at achieving than you probably thought.

Here is a brief list of daily goals that are good building blocks that you may have, or could add, into your daily routine:

- Getting out of bed without hitting snooze.
- Making your bed.
- Finding food for breakfast, from money you earned.
- Getting to school or work on time.
- Being a positive and enthusiastic person.
- Spending some time with a loved one.
- Exercising.

- Getting to bed at a decent time.
- Getting 7-8 hours of restful sleep.
- Keeping your home tidy and clean.

The following is another list of goals you may already have that you may not appreciate as much as you could. They all required a level of effort and determination to reach the end goal and you should be pleased about that.

- Finished secondary school.
- Hired for a job.
- Bought a car.
- Found and moved into own house.
- Have two wonderful friends.
- Raised good kids.
- Slimmed down.
- Travelled somewhere you wanted to go.
- Kept a good eye on personal finances each month.
- Did some charity work.

What we can see from these lists is that a lot of goals are what many people take for granted. They assume they come with their birth certificate. Or perhaps they believe the bar is so low in achieving these they do not even rate them. Perhaps society has dismissed them as so lowly that people just accept that they happen. Of course, this is not true. Especially for the billions of people who know that their very lives depend on their finding nutritious food and clean water just to survive until tomorrow.

So, you are used to setting and achieving goals, even if many of those goals are set and achieved habitually. This proves that goals are easy to understand, set, and achieve. This is even more true when we understand the idea of chunking and how that can greatly improve our ability to succeed and achieve anything.

So the ideas of goal-setting and achievement are easy to understand. This is especially true if you are sporting your growth mindset and prepared to improve your life. Yes, it will take some focus and perseverance. And we also know that we are likely to be a mess before we have success. But if you follow these steps and use the techniques outlined in this book, you will succeed. You will shift from uncomfortable to unstoppable.

IV. Be SMART with your goals

Although we are setting and achieving goals all of the time without even knowing it, we are not gaining skills in the goal arena. The better you understand how goals work, the better you will do in succeeding with your goals.

One reason people don't succeed with less-familiar, higher-level or large goals is they are not fully aware of why easier goals can be achieved. They just do them. However, we need to understand the workings of the goal system so that we can use it fully to our advantage. Playing the game is one thing. But once you understand the intricate rules of a game, your success will flourish.

There are five key components in a goal. These gained in popularity after George T. Dorian outlined them in a November 1981 issue of *Management Review*. For optimal success, S.M.A.R.T. goals should be:

Specific

Measurable

Assignable

Realistic

Time-related

A simple example of how SMART goals can focus your mind and improve the likelihood of success is as follows.

A goal stated without the SMART goal format: *I would like to lose weight.*

A goal stated with the SMART goal format: *I would like to reduce my weight by 23 pounds and weigh 127 pounds by the 24th of December, which is five months from now.*

The benefits

You can see in the second example that there are some clear milestone points in it. It notes how much you have to lose and how many months you have to do it. It also has you focus on the destination, being 127 pounds, so you can be reminding yourself each day what a 127-pound person thinks like, moves like, and is like. The sooner you can re-imagine yourself as a 127-pound person, the sooner you will act like one and reach your goal. Not only that, but after you slim to that level, if you have a new self-image of a 127-pound person, you are much more likely to remain around your new weight target because you believe you belong there and see yourself in that category.

We also note a specific date for your transition to be complete. You'll notice with most things in life that you often need a hard deadline to make things happen. It also helps you to plan for the future. If you are going to reduce your weight by 23 pounds, you are likely to need some new clothes. With the specific date, you will be able to start looking at appropriate clothes for that time of year. You can start looking at various items you will want to buy and put them on your reward list. So as you approach 130, you can simply order a few of those new clothes as your reward. It also helps to confirm your new self-image. These nicely fitting new clothes will confirm to your mind that yes you are a 127-pound person.

Finally, by being specific with your goal, you will start to be able to visualize your goal. The greater the detail with which you can visualize a goal, the more you are bought into it. As you continue to think about the general goal and the detailed specifics, you will start to attract related items into your life. You will start to use the Law of Attraction to your advantage. This Law is the belief that if you think positive or negative thoughts, you will bring positive or negative experiences into your life. Some claim this to be an ESP-like super science using the power of the universe. While this may be true, there are also solid, everyday reasons why the Law of Attraction tends to work.

The more you focus on something, the more you are thinking about it and looking for related items in general. You will normalize it. You will get comfortable with it. You will also begin to notice all the ancillary pieces around it. You will become more aware of the helpful links you have in your current life. For example, say you are interested in buying a new car. Perhaps you fancy a sports car, like a Porsche. As you think more about it, you may start to talk about it with friends. You may even find out one of your work colleagues is a member of a Porsche owners club. Another friend has a friend who is a mechanic at the local Porsche dealership.

As you become more aware of Porsches through magazines, members clubs, test drives, brochures, and YouTube channels, you will become more comfortable with the idea of owning one. As you immerse yourself in the culture of the car and brand, you can shift your self-image so that you start to believe that you are indeed a Porsche owner type of person. You will normalize owning one as your network of Porsche-related people grows and your knowledge and immersion grows. Then you will attract even more people and brand-related experiences into your life as other people start to see you inextricably linked with the brand.

It will all start with recognizing what you want and taking that first step toward achieving it.

KEY POINTS

CHAPTER 8 – SET GOALS

> ‣ Quite possibly, the most important thing you will do in your life is set goals.

> ‣ Remember, there are likely to be many, many individual steps, milestones, or mini goals that need to occur to make the broad goal happen.

> ‣ Larger goals can be broken down into more manageable and discreet component parts – Chunking. This helps us get our mind around the next objective and makes each objective clearer.

> ‣ Goals can act as a compass on the way to another destination where we are not clear on the final outcome.

> ‣ When you complete a task or a goal, it feels good. The more you accomplish, the better you'll feel.

> ‣ When you are specific with your goal, you will start to be able to visualize your goal. The greater the detail with which you can visualize a goal, the more you will buy into it.

STEP 3

ACTIONS... TO HELP YOU *WRITE*

▸ Actually start writing. Put your thoughts in one spot.

▸ Reimagine your future. Write it down. Review the Imagination section in Chapter 6 Section I.

▸ Assess and sort your many ideas for your future and focus on a few for now.

▸ Look at changes in your environment - reduce or replace people or things to help you achieve your goals.

▸ Repeat this saying – "You can't change the people in your life, but you can change the people in your life."

▸ Find people you can learn from and allocate ever-increasing amounts of time with them.

▸ For some quick start help or more information about how to get started, go to www.scottsbook.com/achieveanything/startnow

▸ Write down why you want to do the thing you're thinking about. Then, underneath your answer, write the question Why? Then think about why you want that situation or result. Repeat.

▸ When thinking about your ideas about your future – GO BIGGER!

▸ When setting goals, the secret will be to set and achieve the more significant ones while enjoying your success with the everyday variety too.

‣ Writing out the detailed steps is a process called chunking. Use this method to break your goals down into manageable parts. For more information go to www.scottsbook.com/achieveanything/chunking

‣ It is highly recommended that you acknowledge (write out) your daily successes and celebrate the smaller wins so you build a strong base of achievements.

‣ It is essential that we understand the workings of the goal system so that we can use it fully to our advantage. We need our goals to be Specific, Measurable, Assignable, Realistic and Time-related. (SMART). For more information go to www.scottsbook.com/achieveanything/smartgoals

STEP 4 - **PLAN**

"Nobody ever wrote down a plan to be broke, fat, lazy or stupid. Those things are what happen when you don't have a plan."

–Larry Winget

I know you are the type of person who is going to succeed in many things, if:

A. You are still with me, and
B. You have done every exercise I've noted so far in this book (at least once!)

If you have made it this far in the book and have done what is noted in B) above, you're going to love this next bit. This is where the future successful people move a little closer to becoming unstoppable. This is where those with powerful and well-articulated mental and physical stamina take a turn at the fork in the road and go for gold. This is you. I know you still have the energy and pace to continue. So, let's go!

If you want to achieve anything, then you will need to do the following:

- Learn the process.
- Follow the process. Exactly.
- Continue to do this daily.
- Find a better process.
- Repeat steps above.

Take the same steps even if it gets a little boring, repeating the same things over and over. Repetition is the mother of all learning. And perseverance will be rewarded with compounded gains.

> *"If you don't design your own life plan, chances are you'll fall into someone else's plan. And guess what they have planned for you? Not much."*

> **–Jim Rohn**

You see the same issue with New Year's resolutions and most projects people begin. The excitement of doing something new carries people through at the beginning. The newness is so exciting and palpable that it is easy to get up and get out of bed early every day and work on these changes until late at night and sometimes until early in the morning. You can get such incredible joy and momentum from the progress you are making and it all seems to be happening with ease. But frequently, after one, two, or three weeks, something gives. The newness has worn off. You haven't achieved your major goal yet. Even though you didn't expect to yet, you sure wish it was that quick and easy. In addition, your momentum, stamina, and will power will be fading away.

This inflection point helps people to better understand how much they really want that goal. It also gets you very clear on whether your Why is big enough. By the third week of January, most people — I've heard it is 82% — have given up on their New Year's resolutions. They have slipped back into their old habits, lost the drive, are too tired, and don't have the time anymore. Sometimes it is all too much, and for others, something more exciting, novel, or unique has taken its place.

If you have a very clear and big enough purpose or Why, you will find a way to keep going. You will not let missing one day slow you down. You will not let any setbacks slow you down or stop you. You are becoming unstoppable.

You also have to develop a consistent daily habit of output. Set aside 30 minutes each day in your diary. Start with five very focused minutes, if that is truly all you can fit in at the moment. Do this every single day. Don't break the chain. Put it in the calendar at the same early morning time every day so you are sure to get it done. Use the Seven Day Success Cycle tactic we outline later in this section (Chapter 10, section III).

You need to make this action a must in your life, like eating. Tony Robbins says we get our musts. We want to get our "shoulds" too, but few people get their "shoulds." "Shoulds" tend to roll off the back of the truck and end up in the ditch. So, upgrade your most important "shoulds" to a *MUST* and start getting them fully done. You will succeed!

Chapter 9. Understand clearly where you are

So now that you've decided what you want, we have to find out where you are. Where are you starting from? What resources are at your disposal? How far along in the process are you already? Starting from a different position or perspective will often mean taking a different route to the same destination.

If you want to get to London, you'll have a different plan of action and timeframe if you're starting in New York rather than Paris.

Securing and using your journal

So, let's take stock and become aware of where we are now. Oh, and let's not just think about it. Let's get a pen or pencil and some paper (or a device) and write this information down. Ideally, you would put this into your new goal journal. That's right. Time for an upgrade. No longer will you have pieces of paper floating around or being misplaced. Get down to the shops and buy one or order one online! Then you can always remember the day you started and where you are right now. This will also make it easier to track, monitor, and analyze your progress. This is a lot easier than it sounds and requires only a few minutes each day.

You will also be able to go back a month from now, a year from now or even 10 years from now and see where this all started. Then you can look back and see where you were, what the steps you took were, and realize how far you've progressed and how many goals you have achieved! You will, of course, be very proud of the journey you've been on and grateful for the journey and the results you will be enjoying.

This is part of celebrating your efforts and success and reminding yourself how far you've come.

So you need to buy a journal! Ideally this is some sort of bound book that you can write in and keep with you to add the information about your goal, actions required, and achievements along the way. If you don't have a journal already, mark it in your diary to buy one. Note down which day, time, and location you are going to buy one. Once you have your book, open it up and put the date and time at the top of the page. Make this a habit so you can always go back and track where you were, what you were thinking, and when it was. You will smile at the things you wrote, what you thought was important, sweet things about your family and memories of what you did. A real treasure to keep for life. It's also an amazing tool to help you focus and achieve anything.

Assess the brutal facts of reality

Now, on that piece of paper you have, write down the relevant details related to your priority goal. If you are trying to lose weight/become slimmer/be fitter, then you should write down where you are with the metrics that you want to change. By metrics, I simply mean the items you would like to change that can be objectively/factually measured. For example, perhaps you would like your weight to go from 175 pounds to 150 pounds. Perhaps you want to drop a dress or trouser size, or two, from a size 14 dress down to 10 or size 34 trousers down to 30. Perhaps you would like your biceps to measure 15 inches in circumference. Measure your key metric areas now. No need to be shy or nervous. You already know where you are, generally, and so does everyone else. These are your brutal facts of reality. And they will continue to be until you acknowledge them. Now write it down in your journal. For the more tech-inclined, you can do this in a Notes app in your phone. With it in your phone, you will have it with you most of the time for review and adding information on the go. Personally, I do both.

Additionally, if you want to improve your finances, you can use the same tactic. In order to get on top of your expenses, or earn more money, first start by assessing where you are today. How much do you have in savings, debt, investments and what is the income from your various income sources? Then consider where you would like to be with each of those items in 3 months, 6, 12, 24 and 60 months (5 years). There are lots of books, websites, YouTube videos and coaches to help you get on a better financial track than you are on now. Start looking at your finances for 5 minutes each day. Focus on your improvements and work toward your wealth goal each day.

You can do this exercise with any goal. Whether you want to write a book, get a promotion, be fitter or healthier, create passive income, be a better parent, daughter, or son, or even just improve how you spend your evenings.

For each goal, remember to note down the facts and then accept them. There is no need to subjectively comment or judge the facts. It's of no use to dismiss them, reject them, or misconstrue them. Simply note the facts down in an objective, third-party way. Once you have these facts, find a source that will provide objective statistics about the goal. Gather some information as to what is normal, good, bad, or excellent. Then you can start benchmarking your facts against what others have as their facts. You can use these details to understand the potential for improvement that appears ahead of you.

Getting started

Simply think of the basic metrics you want to shift, or the parts of the goal you want to achieve. Then assess where you are now. As noted earlier, use chunking as it makes goal achievement easier to do and you can actually see yourself completing the smaller steps.

You can go to the website, www.scottsbook.com/achieveanything/startnow, where you will find some lists of the more common goals.

I know some people might struggle at this point to acknowledge and measure their basic metrics. If you are struggling with getting the basic metrics, or parts of the goal, down on a piece of paper, or in a journal, then reflect on what is holding you back. Frequently, your challenge will be things like fear, embarrassment, or feeling silly as you might not want this information in writing. You may be concerned someone will find this information, though they often already know it. Perhaps you're having a bout of perfectionism, or you just don't know whether you're on the right track and doing this correctly. Well, you don't have to write it down. Though, it is strongly recommended.

One way to look at it is that you are facing up to your challenge and writing this information down will help you face the brutal facts of reality. Another consideration is that we rarely like the medicine but if that is the best prescription, we may as well use it.

My own working example

Let's say it's a fitness goal you have. So currently you weigh 190 pounds. You have a 36-inch waist and those are the basic metrics you want to focus on. Now decide where you would like to get to. For example, 160 pounds and a 31-inch waist might be your optimal goal. So first, you need to reduce your weight by 30 pounds. By doing so, this should also reduce your waist size by the five inches you are looking for. Now you can add a bunch of other metrics such as bicep size, abs visibility, neck size, thigh size, clothing size (brand dependent), walking a mile without stopping, jogging five km in less than 30 minutes, etc. But if you've got the main couple of metrics to focus on, that is enough to get started. What you want to do is get a couple of metrics written down, roughly, right now. Do not spend time researching the different possible and ideal metrics. You don't want the Law of Diminishing Intent to get in your way.

So, when I wanted to lose some weight, I looked at where I was, took the two basic items, my weight, and my waist size, and asked myself a question: How do I get to be 155 pounds and a 31-inch waist? I then decided I wanted to reach that goal as quickly as I could, which was four months in my mind. I was 175 pounds and a 34-inch waist at the end of December 2015. I'd taken greater notice of my body size after a big Christmas period of food and drink and inactivity. Up until that point, I had never really considered my weight, as I was always quite fit, healthy, and active. But I was wearing trousers with a size 34-inch waist and I thought to myself, "why should I be size 34 when I was size 30/31 in my teens and early 20s. Why can't I be that size again? Just because I'm older? No way! Nonsense. So I went from 175 pounds down to 155 pounds in less than two months. And my waist dropped from size 34 to size 30/31.

I felt I may have become too slim but I was getting a lot of compliments and I felt really good about being at a good, healthy size for my height and body structure. Not quite the fitness level of the Ultimate Fighting Champion (UFC) guys who got me motivated, but fairly fit.

UFC fighting fit

You see, what made me realize I could be lighter and fitter was something that happened to me one night while watching a few minutes of tv. At the time, I wasn't watching much television anymore, but I had turned it on for a five-minute channel surf to see just what kind of things were on. I came across a UFC weigh-in. Now these two fighters were in phenomenal shape and I realized they were the same height as me and they were in fighting-fit form. Clearly, they were quite tough guys too. Then I realized their weight. They weighed about 155 pounds. That set me on the path to achieving the weight, waist size, and fitness goals that I had been thinking about. Rather than "getting smaller," "looking weaker," I had some powerful, tough guy examples at that weight and size to use as role models. I had been a little challenged, in my beliefs, with being a smaller size (like small and medium shirts instead of medium and large) but now I would be at "my fighting weight" and be «fighting fit." Instead of feeling like I was shrinking or weakening, I felt a new-found awareness which brought a feeling of personal power and control over the fitness aspects of my life.

James Bond

Soon after, I saw a picture of 007, James Bond, in a magazine and I asked myself, "Why couldn't I be the same size as James Bond?" That would be another great mental comparison I could hold onto. It would be a great mental brand association to make me want to achieve it more. So I searched online for Daniel Craig and found his weight and waist metrics. I found out that he was the same height as me and he had the same waist size I wanted. In addition, he was a similar age to me, so he became my avatar. I then printed out a picture of Mr. Bond, at his fittest, and used that with the UFC visualization whenever I needed to remind myself where I was headed. This really works exceptionally well! Adding the picture to my vision board and using the visualization technique, I had a clear view of where I wanted to go and focused on that daily. By not thinking about where I was or had been, but rather consistently focusing on where I wanted to go, I was able to quickly get the results I wanted.

I. Note the precise distance and direction you need to travel

Precision can be annoying and pedantic. I get it. However, when setting out to solve a problem or reach a goal, precision will be your new best friend. Imagine, polar explorers setting out to reach the North Pole by generally heading north for a wee bit. You may never hear from them again. Not provisioning correctly for the distance or duration could be deadly. And of course they could go north but narrowly miss their desired goal of being the first to the pole (magnetic or true north). That would be massively disappointing after all the energy, time, and resources put into the quest.

Just like you and your goals, you will want to achieve them, not simply, "have a go." So the more precise you can be with the detail of your desired goal, the more likely you will prepare accordingly and therefore the greater your possibility, and probability, of success.

So get very precise with measuring where you are now with respect to your goal. Write this information down in your journal with today's date above it. This is your starting point.

If your goal is to get slimmer and fitter, measure your key body parts like waist, biceps, and thighs. Then write out specifically what you would like those metrics to change to and by what specific date. Now you simply need to follow one of the many plans that exist for your area of focus or goal. This is how you make your plan complete. Just like planning a holiday or a visit with your Mom. You can make it super-complicated and add levels of complexity. However, you can also keep it simple, stick to the plan, and shift from uncomfortable to unstoppable.

KEY POINTS

CHAPTER 9 – UNDERSTAND CLEARLY WHERE YOU ARE

- ‣ If you have a very clear and big enough purpose or Why, you will find a way to keep going. You will not let missing one day slow you down. You will not let any setbacks slow you down or stop you.

- ‣ Start with one to five very focused (timed) minutes a day for self improvement. Do this everyday. Never miss twice.

- ‣ Where are you starting from?

- ‣ Be brutally honest with yourself. Be kind with the delivery though. No need to judge, comment or note any reasons.

- ‣ A new perspective can greatly impact your feeling of personal power to improve results.

- ‣ The more precise you can be with the detail of your desired goal, the more likely you will prepare accordingly and therefore the greater your possibility, and probability, of success.

Chapter 10. Prioritize and structure goals

So you know where you are and you know where you want to be. This is an excellent start. Now you also realize you have many goals that you would like to work on to achieve successful outcomes. Because of that, we have a little more work to do.

Prioritize

We need to look at all of the goals you have written down and decide which five are the most important to us right now. You see, we cannot focus if we have 10 or 15 goals we are working on at the same time. In addition, everything takes longer than we expect in the short run. Part of the reason for the extra time is the extra reading, thinking, and learning we have to do while trying to make progress in new areas we are not so familiar with. Even if we have some familiarity but not pro-level amounts, we will still need to invest more of our time to improve our awareness and skills. We need to factor that in, or we can become discouraged by the constant gap between expectations and reality with respect to our time, skills, and progress.

Take the time now to quickly look through your goals and put a 1 next to all of your highest priority goals. Put a 2 next to those you think are secondary as they are less urgent and less important to you compared to the goals with a 1 next to them.

You may have more than five with a 1 next to it. That is ok. Have a second look through the 1 list and see if you can make some into 2s. With the remaining 1s, quantify them. Consider the amount of time and effort they may take and whether they would fit in your life at the moment. Goals which can be very time intensive, such as building another income stream in your life, can be left until after you get a few quicker, easier wins or less time-intensive goals completed. For example, if walking four days per week for 20 minutes is a goal, set that up first and get it going. Beginning this habit should be easier than other options, so you can build up a little momentum with your success. You will see that you are moving in the direction you want and be inspired to continue forward.

I. Timeframes for each goal — day, week, month, year

Take a look at your shortlist of 1s again. Write down next to each of the goals the amount of time you think it will take to do them. Note down the actual time required by you as the first metric. This may be 200 hours. Then note down how much time lapse you expect there to be between the start and finish. For example, it may take 20 weeks working at 10 hours a week or roughly 90 minutes per day. Or you may require others to be involved, which can also take time, though not your time. It might be a situation whereby you apply for permission or acceptance, such as for a housing development or a university degree. You can't know how long these responses will take to come back, but you can ask for an indication or make an informed guess.

So, if you can allocate 60 minutes per day, five days per week, that's a start. Then, you may know there will be two required gaps of time where you wait for others to get back to you, each taking two weeks. Now we can calculate that your new goal would take about 44 weeks from the time you start. (60 minutes = 1 hour × 5 days per week × 40 weeks = 200 hours + 2 sets of 2 gap weeks = 44 weeks in total).

Start and finish

Now that you know the required time and elapsed time estimates, I suggest you add a contingency time amount. I suggest adding a 50% increase to the required time and the waiting-for-others estimate. In the case above, that would be 200 hours plus 100 hours (50%) which comes to 300 hours. The two-week turnaround times should be increased by one week for both instances. That would put you at 300 hours and six weeks of waiting time. Your new time estimate is now 60 weeks of your effort (with 1 hour x 5 days per week) and 6 weeks of waiting for others. This comes to a total of 66 weeks.

This is a good practice as people are not very good at estimating time factors and few people have the will or accountability to power through something in the most efficient timeframe.

You should now note down the start date of each project (day, month, year) and the expected finish date. You may be able to do it in your original timeframe, however, this method removes some of the stress of the expectations v reality gap. If you do finish early, or within your original estimate, that is great and should be celebrated. If you work to the extended time period, then you will still be fine.

Once you have the dates at either end noted down for each goal, then add in the time when you will start and complete the project. The more precise you can be, the more real this will become and the more excitement you will have for the goal and accomplishing it. You may decide that you will start at 19:10 on your first day, once you are back from work and the house is quiet. Your project completion date might be on a Saturday and you will target a 09:45 (a.m.) time so that you can have the afternoon to go and celebrate your great victory.

Also note down on the paper what would have to change on a weekly, and also daily, basis to complete a straight line to move from here to there. For example, what used to occupy that 45 or 60 minutes per day that you are saying you will now allocate to this new goal? Was it the news, a tv show, or random scrolling on social media? Whatever it was, you need to be clear to yourself that that is no longer the activity for that timeframe in the day. Remember to set up your environment to make the old habit hard or unpleasant and the new habit easy and enjoyable. This will help you greatly in the first few sessions.

Remind yourself often

> *"People often say that motivation doesn't last.*
> *Neither does bathing - that's why we recommend*
> *it daily"*
>
> **–Zig Ziglar**

Finally, think of where you will put these written plans so you are reminded of them frequently each day. You could put your two-page plan on your laptop so when you sit in front of it in the morning to start your day, it is the first thing you read and review. Also, when you finish for the day, you need to put it back on your laptop. This is a good time to refresh those goal plans before your laptop, and you, go to sleep.

You can also post your goals around the house on little recipe cards so you can see them when you shave, shower, get dressed, brush your hair or teeth, and open the fridge. The more frequently you see your goal, the more exposure you have to it. With this greater exposure, you should become more familiar and comfortable with it. Then you should start to internalize it and accept it is happening. This will become a good positive feedback loop until you accelerate into success. That is how you will continue to shift from uncomfortable to unstoppable.

II. MTO (Minimum, Target, Outrageous)

There is a great way to look at goal-setting that few people use. I first saw it explained very well in a book written by Canadian author and businessman, Raymond Aaron. The book was called, *Double Your Income Doing What You Love."* There were a number of great ideas in the book and this MTO method of goal-setting was one of them.

The idea is that you set three levels of *measurable* results for your goal rather than just one big one (Measurable is the M in SMART goals as outlined above in chapter 8). This way, you can be pleased by getting some result rather than disappointed because you didn't achieve the big goal you wanted.

For example, let's say that you wanted to give your bedroom a clear out and make it look sharp. Rather than having the room fully sorted out, including decluttered, repainted, and everything placed well, you could have three tiers. First tier that you would be happy with would be the minimum. This should be something that you are going to achieve with very little effort and time. This is something that you will be pleased to have completed as a minimum. In this example, it might be decluttering your desktop. So, no matter what, when you go to work on improving your room, if all you manage to complete in the time allocated is decluttering your desktop, you will be delighted.

The next tier is the actual target that you would really like to achieve. This target may include decluttering your desktop but also the desk drawers, your closet, chest of drawers, your floor, bed and shelves. This would be a huge win for you if you completed all these items in the time allocated. You would have succeeded with your minimum goal and your target goal. What a great feeling that would be!

Finally, you could also set an outrageous goal. This level of goal is the ultimate one. This would be the culmination of all the possible things you could imagine getting done. So, of course it would include the minimum and target results but also a variety of other ideal results. In this example, that may include painting the walls your favorite color, getting some wonderful curtains up, replacing the carpet on the floor, and getting your two favorite pictures framed and positioned nicely on the wall.

The reason for the outrageous goal is to keep your maximizing mind on the possibilities that exist to bring you joy. You may not achieve all of those extras, but what if you achieved just one or two of them? Wouldn't that feel good to meet your target and get a few extra bonus results? However, if you didn't get any of the outrageous items, you wouldn't feel disappointed because you did achieve your target goal.

Try using this technique each time you set out to achieve a goal. You will develop it as a habit and I think you will feel better for it. As with anything, it has its pros and cons, but it is one of the best ways to manage stress due to the expectation versus reality gap.

III. The 7-Day Success Cycle

The 7-Day Success Cycle is a significant enabler of success. It is my simple yet highly effective strategy that will greatly help you achieve anything. I have successfully used this technique to write this book, prepare for marathons, and build a strong morning routine to invigorate the start of my day.

The 7-Day Success Cycle is as simple as getting a time and topic into your calendar for each of the coming seven days. Pick your project start date. For this exercise, we will assume it is a Sunday. Decide on a 30-minute "prep time" slot during the day when you can map out your week ahead with respect to your new goal. Put that prep time slot into your diary now and set a timer to remind you. This can be five minutes at first, if that is all the time you can allocate. However, you can build up to 30 minutes per day as quickly as you can.

When the 30-minute slot arrives, stop everything you are doing and focus 100% on your goal and the activities you must do in the week ahead to move closer to it. For each of the next seven days, you must select a 30-minute "do time." You will also need one additional 30-minute "prep time" slot on the seventh day so that you can plan the following week ahead. Put the date and the start and finish time in your calendar along with one or two things you need to action for each slot. Additionally, set an alarm on your phone to remind you about each appointment. The time of day you block out can be different each day, although it helps with simplicity and consistency if the time is the same each day.

You must consistently and diligently work on your project at the allotted time each day. With each daily activity, you will gain greater momentum, confidence, pride, knowledge, and enthusiasm. Not only will you be one or two steps closer to your goal every day, but you will start tuning in to some luck. As the golfer, Jack Nicklaus, once said, "The harder I work, the luckier I get." Some say it is karma, while others might suggest it is the Law of Attraction at work. Regardless of why it is happening, or what you call it, press on!

If you can build your habit so that you strictly follow The 7-Day Success Cycle every day going forward, you will become an unstoppable, goal-achieving master.

Why this method works is that it combines all of the seven steps highlighted in this book. You need to **Think** about what you are going to focus on for the week. Then you'll have to **Overcome** your own challenges, such as time and competing priorities. From there you need to **Write** in the times and activities for each day. You will use this tool and others, to put a **Plan** in place. Each day, these time slots will force you to **Act** and produce something which hopefully will bring about the outcomes you are targeting. You will also **Review** your progress either daily or weekly and hopefully both. Finally, you can **Celebrate** your daily discipline, wins, developing habits and weekly achievements.

By following this method for the weeks ahead, you will ingrain these steps into your personal system and they will become habits. This will help you achieve anything as you begin to use these simple steps more frequently and easily.

KEY POINTS

CHAPTER 10 – PRIORITIZE AND STRUCTURE GOALS

> ‣ At this stage, you know where you are and you know where you want to be. You also realize you have many goals that you would like to work on to achieve successful outcomes.

> ‣ Get an easy goal going first so you can build a habit and feel good about your commitment and success.

- Get very clear on your time factors of when and how long.

- Note down what you will remove from your schedule to add this new goal in.

- Set up your environment to make the old habit hard or unpleasant and the new habit easy or enjoyable, or both!

- The MTO method for goal setting. The idea is that you set three levels of results for your goal rather than just one big one. This way, you can be pleased by getting some result rather than disappointed because you didn't achieve the big goal you wanted.

- The 7-Day Success Cycle is a significant enabler of success. You must consistently and diligently work on your project at the allotted time each day. With each daily activity, you will gain greater momentum, confidence, pride, knowledge, and enthusiasm. This method also combines all the 7 steps highlighted in this book.

Chapter 11. Map key activities and milestones

Two things that can radically transform your life and results are mapping and tracking. We will look into the mapping component here in this brief chapter. The tracking section will be covered in more detail in Chapter 15.

What is mapping? It is the act of filling in the detail like creating a map. It shows where you are and where you want to be and what you need to go through to move from here to there.

Why is mapping so important? Well it serves a number of purposes. The three most important reasons why you want to spend some time on mapping are the following:

- **Route to Results:** Mapping helps you get a better understanding of the path to x or the route to results. By going through the mapping process, you will tease out some of the details you might not have realized are required steps to reach your goal.
- **Second time swifter:** Once your mind has seen how to do something once, it is usually quicker and easier the second time. You'll have noticed this when going somewhere new by car, foot, bike, or airplane. It is a near certainty that your initial journey seems to take forever or longer than anticipated. However, your journey home and the next time you make the trip, the time seems much quicker and the route easier to find. So, by mapping out your journey in the first place, even if it is bit of guesswork, you will make it seem a lot easier when you actually go through the process.
- **Mapping for tracking:** If you have mapped out a route, it is a lot easier to review it and track whether you are on course or not. This is one of the chief differentiators

between successful and unsuccessful projects. If you don't know where you are going, how will you know you are on the right track for success? The tracking allows you to see if you go off course and allows you to course-correct early. Early detection and correction are helpful in saving time and money while avoiding unnecessary challenges.

How to map

I have found mapping to be easier if you write out some key steps by hand, or on a device right at the beginning. It goes back to the idea of using your imagination or brainstorming. The first couple of steps might take a moment to get down but then hopefully you will enter a state of flow and the ideas and steps will come to you quite quickly. Sometimes I find I cannot write the points down fast enough to keep up with my mind.

This step is easier if you a) know where you are starting from, b) know where you are trying to get to, and c) have some general idea of what your first or next step is. So, referencing back to the work you have already done in this book, get clear on the destination, your departure point, and one of any of the next steps you could take. Remember to begin with the end in mind.

As an example, using the lettering above, imagine you will be heading to the airport in a few days for an important flight. Perhaps you will be taking a car to the airport (a) in order to board a specific flight (b). You need to be quite clear on the date and time of arrival at the airport. And you also need to be clear on the boarding and departure time of the flight. You want to easily and calmly make it on your flight. Knowing that is your intention, you need to go back and decide on your first step (c). This might be making a phone call and booking a taxi to the airport that will have you there with plenty of time to spare.

Focus on one thing

It is amazing how focusing on the most important thing each day can make a world of difference. Once again, it pays to be specific and not general. You are going to make the most headway each day when you focus on that one thing that is essential to be done and will move you closer to your goal, more than anything else will.

To illustrate this, let's assume you own a bakery. What is the one thing that is essential and will make the biggest difference to your business? On most days, that is going to be baking goods for sale. Accounting can wait, fixing the website can wait, and painting the delivery truck can wait. They are all important, but without goods for sale, you won't need a truck, website, or accountant.

Another day you may hear that a shop is available for sale in the next town. As you have been looking to add another shop, you think this is good news. Therefore, making a phone call to the shop owner or broker is your essential item for that day. Although you should still get your own shop open with goods baked and ready for sale, this phone call becomes the potential game-changer priority as your "essential to do today" item. You need to be prepared and to pounce every day on the most critical matter in your life or business.

There are several books that cover this important point in much more detail. You will find it covered in different ways in *The One Thing, Essentialism* and *Eat That Frog* by Brian Tracy. One of the key differences between the books is that *Eat That Frog* is more focused on first doing the thing on your to do list which you like the least, so the rest of the items seem easy in comparison.

Be clear and specific

Life becomes so much easier when you become clear on what you want. If you know the item you want to purchase when in a store, ask for it specifically. When you want to go to the British Museum for an afternoon, don't wistfully mention to your friends that you would like to spend some time reflecting on history. You may be given a book rather than be taken to the museum. Finally, when you know you would like to work in an industry or specific company, be sure to tell people exactly that. They are more likely to be able to help you if they know precisely what it is you are looking for.

This is true of gifts for birthdays, Christmas, and other significant events during the year. It is great when people can be clear about what they specifically want. That way you spend less time thinking about (and anxiously considering) what they would like or would suit them.

Top tip. Get clear on three gifts you would appreciate at three different price points. This could be a paperback or hardcover book, tickets for an event, or a convertible sports car. Then if anyone asks you what you would like for your birthday, you have a few ideas to hand at various price points. And remember our MTO discussion. Putting something on your wish list that is seemingly outrageous to you as a gift may be the perfect price in someone else's mind. Either way, remember to say thank you.

Finally, ensure you note down specific dates and times. This is a great habit to get into. There are so many distractions in the world and time can move on swiftly if you are not paying attention. Time and dates are great for marking deadlines.

They are super for tracking and accountability measures. Use these universal tools to your benefit rather than to your detriment. Work with dates and times to motivate you and keep you on track for your goal. Be the master of time, not its subordinate. You will achieve more, and more quickly. That is why the following phrase was created, "If you need something done, give it to a busy person."

KEY POINTS

CHAPTER 11 – MAP KEY ACTIVITIES AND MILESTONES

- ‣ Mapping and tracking can radically transform your life and results.

- ‣ Mapping shows you the route to results. Like a treasure map.

- ‣ Mapping benefits from "second time swifter" as once your mind has seen how to do something once, it is usually quicker and easier the second time.

- ‣ Map so you can track. It is a lot easier to track your progress if you have a map to follow.

- ‣ Mapping is a lot easier if you a) know where you are, b) know where you are trying to get to, and c) know what your next step is or could be.

- ‣ Do the one essential thing first in your day, especially if don't want to do it.

- ‣ Being clear and specific about your goal or idea usually makes life much easier.

- ‣ Note down dates and times for all goal setting activity.

STEP 4

ACTIONS... TO HELP YOU *PLAN*

- You need to begin by determining where are you starting from? Starting from a different position or perspective will often mean taking a different route to the same destination.

- But a nice journal and start using it to write down your plans today.

- Write down your starting place, time and date so you can look back and see where you were, what the steps you took were, and realize how far you progressed and how many goals you achieved!

- Measure your key metric areas now!

- Be clear which ones you want to shift and by what amount.

- Chunk the goals down into smaller steps and success milestones.

- You can go to the website, www.scottsbook.com/achieveanything/startnow where you will find some lists of the more common goals.

- Prioritize your goals and add time frames with contingency lapses.

- Write down your goals and put a 1 or a 2 next to them. Aim for no more than five 1's.

- Ensure you have great exposure to your goal by making it visible around the house. This will allow you to become more familiar and comfortable with it and you should start to internalize it and accept it is happening. This will become a good positive feedback loop until you accelerate into success. Put down the book and do this now.

▸ You must get clear on the destination of your goal, your departure point, and one of any of the next steps you could take.

▸ Focus on the most important thing each day to obtain your goal.

STEP 5 - **ACT**

This step is where things really start to happen. The first and second steps in the book were more about preparation and therefore cerebral (Think, Overcome), while steps three and four focused more on visual intent (Write, Plan). This step, in the process of achievement, has us focus our time and efforts on executing and the challenges and habits associated with that.

We are now moving from preparation to actually making things happen! This can be terrifying for some people and very exciting for others. Usually these feelings arise for a similar reason. That is, we are now going to make this happen!

This means we have to look like we are trying to succeed and achieve something important to us. This also means we might slip, perform poorly, fail or get socially and publicly uncomfortable.

Yes. That could happen. But we know this matter is important to us. So we need to see past the initial challenges and see ourselves delighted on the other side of those challenges. This is where our strong Why comes in. It will shelter us from the feelings of struggle. It will help us get through the difficult part at the start.

So let's dive into these chapters, study the elements of action-taking and get things moving forward.

Ready? Action!

Chapter 12. Decision, Commitment, Resolve: Until!

Opportunities appear after a decision is made.

Decision

It is incredible what can happen once you have made a decision. Your life can change instantly! I am sure you can think of times when you had clarity of thought and knew exactly what you were trying to achieve and then made the decision to do it. This may have been an event such as whether to take a certain job or course at school. It may have been with respect to a relationship, health and fitness, or your family. It may involve buying something such as clothes on holiday or a car that you love or need. Certainly, if you've ever purchased a house, you know what it's like to have made that decision.

Commitment

Always following a real, committed decision you will find action driving you toward achieving the outcome the decision was targeting. So if you were buying a house, you may find the action that came after the decision was calling the agent, putting an offer on that house, or signing the documents to complete the purchase of the house. If it was buying clothes, the action may have been taking the clothes to the counter for purchase. Of course, the real decision feeling may have come when you handed over your credit or debit card or when they put it through and there was no turning back. It's at these moments where we feel certainty (sometimes mixed with fear) that this is the direction we want to take, and we commit ourselves to that direction or outcome. This is when we commit ourselves, truly commit ourselves, and decide there is no turning back.

Resolve

This certainty of feeling is very exciting and empowering because this decision and commitment you have made helps to bring you toward the vision you have for your life: the clear vision you have. Usually, to make a decision we need clarity, though not always. Sometimes we have to make a decision with only 70% of the information, a general vision, and the end goal. Occasionally we have even less visibility and because of a time pressure, external factor, or general uncertainty that low visibility won't improve. In these moments, we need to make a decision, commit to the best possible route that we can see at the moment, and be prepared to adjust as we move toward our goal. When you are fully committed to your decision, you should resolve that you will not stop until you have achieved the objective. This powerful resolve helps you to overcome any obstacles there will be during the process of trying to achieve your goal. Of course, it is so much easier to decide, commit, and resolve if you are clear on your strongest and most powerful Why.

This new resolve to achieve your goal reminds me of what Jim Rohn said in the 80s (1980s for those of you reading this well into the future). He said that when you resolve to do something, and are fully committed to your decision, you will not stop *until* you achieve the goal. The word until is such a powerful word. I will not rest *until* I have completed this race. I will continue to press forward *until* my income is where I want it to be.

The power of words

Can you remember ever saying these words: I have decided. I am committed. I resolve. I will continue until. These are some of the most powerful phrases in the human vocabulary. The word until has helped win wars, discover new places, eliminate disease, reduce hunger and poverty, and it has also driven incredible technological advances such as the airplane, the rocket ship, and the mobile phone. These were all simply mental battles fought and won by committed individuals or groups of people. They had resolved that they would continue the battle to win, *until* they were victorious and had achieved the outcome they had laid out and committed to achieve.

Ideas and dreams

Many people, thousands and possibly millions of people, had probably hoped and dreamed through history about having an "airplane" or some nifty device that could transport them from one place on the planet to another, quickly, safely and easily. Certainly, millions of people had thought how wonderful it would be to be able to communicate with relatives or friends in distant cities and countries on different continents or simply just down the road. We had even seen these ideas used in the future during movies like Star Wars and tv shows such as Star Trek. The creators and writers of that incredible tv show gave us that "swish swish" of automatic sliding doors, the communicator device, and being beamed up or beamed down (which people were still working on and getting closer to, at the time of writing this).

Decisive actions

So, it's not just in the thinking of things that makes them happen. It is in the effort of doing, while being committed, *until* you make the thing happen. I would guess that many people in history had wished for something like a "mobile phone." However, it took a few people, with the resolve to continue, to press forward with actions until they achieved their objective. They had a vision *and* took action. It is these tenacious people who we thank for their resolve and commitment because they are the ones who brought so many of the world's greatest dreams into reality.

Dreamers, imaginers, and idea machines are so important in coming up with incredible concepts and ideas for the future. But even they need to take some action to make their dream a reality. They can take the actions themselves. However, if they don't initiate the action themselves, they need to communicate to others who will. For if they do not take action, or communicate to others what their vision is, they may pass away before their dream is realized. This reminds me of a popular song by the Cooper Brothers where part of the chorus reveals that, "the dream never dies, only the dreamer."

It is truly amazing what we can dream of when we allow ourselves the full range of imagination and openness, and state what we really want in our lives. It is incredible to consider what people can achieve when they set their minds to it. Everything begins in the mind. From the mind we develop awareness. With that awareness we can then have vision. And if that vision is sufficiently inspiring, and fulfils our purpose, we will then make decisions, commit, and resolve to make these things happen.

But with all these things we need the right mindset. We need to be able to let our minds be open to that which we don't have, or don't see, and that which we aren't already. We must open our minds to the possibility of being, doing, or having the many things that our mind is open to considering. Then we need to have the mindset to move these thoughts forward with our own actions or communicate these thoughts to others, so they take the appropriate action and move us closer to the world we want to live in.

KEY POINTS

CHAPTER 12 – DECISION, COMMITMENT, RESOLVE: UNTIL!

›   Decisions you make determine the outcome in your life.

›   Commitment is what proves you are serious about your decision.

   Resolve, or promise yourself, you'll continue and follow through.

›   I have decided. I am committed. I resolve. I will continue until. These are some of the most powerful phrases in the human vocabulary.

Chapter 13. Act as if

When we ACT, our Actions Copy Target.

Acting as if is fascinating. It is the idea of acting as if you have already accomplished something or you are already the somebody you want to be.

People also talk about be, do, have, in this context. The idea that you first decide, in your mind, what you would like to *be* and then you *do* things that being that way would compel you to do (act as if). It stands to reason that then you will have what that type of person would have (e.g. corporate title, a skillset, wealth, fitness level).

For example, what would happen if you were to act as if you were an incredibly successful sports personality. How would you work? How would you speak? Move? Who would you be associating with? What would be important to you every day? What would your day look like? How would you stand? If you start to act and be that person, you should become like that person and adopt their habits, actions, and mannerisms and this should lead you to having their successes too.

Once you act as if you are someone, by adopting the characteristics, habits, and thoughts of that person, you will be very much like that person. So, you will first "be" in your mind, then you will "do" in the physical world and then, due to cause and effect, you will "have" the results that are very similar, or the same, as the person you are emulating. Children can be great at doing this while role-playing at Halloween and actors are so convincing when they do this well.

Let's use the example of wanting a new job in your company. This promotion would be a great step up on the career ladder for you. The best and quickest way to get selected for the role is to act as if you already have the role and do the things someone successful in that role would do. This will require extra work on your part, take more time, and be a challenge while balancing your current duties. However, if you truly are acting as if you are the successful appointee in that role, the probability of being selected for that role will greatly increase. By "being" the appointee in advance, you will do what a successful appointee would do. Your boss and peers will easily see you in the role and you will soon have that promotion.

> *"All the world's indeed a stage, and we are merely players,*
> *Performers and portrayer, each another's audience,*
> *outside the gilded cage."*

–Rush

It is such a simple idea and yet it is so powerful. We see actors use it to great effect on the tv, the big stage, and the silver screen. In fact, there is even a specific way to rehearse, called method acting, that some of the best actors who ever lived have used to great effect. Method acting is an emotion-oriented technique that encourages sincere performances. It is a way of using the actor's mind to get into the specific role in character by living and thinking as if they really were that character or person, in the same circumstances that the other person would have been in. The actor can also call upon their own similar experiences and use these to give a more realistic interpretation for the scene. This can supercharge their acting and their portrayal can be so incredibly believable. You can really notice the difference when someone pretends to be a character and when an actor becomes a character. For example, when someone pretends to be a slimmer or fitter person versus a person who has decided that they are a person who is slim and fit. The first may go through the motions of having to eat less and move more. The latter actually sees themselves as a slim and fit person who happens to be carrying extra weight. So it is easy for that person to eat less and move more because that is who they are. Their self-image has changed, not just their short-term actions. From the moment you decide to act as if, the results you will have will be truly astounding.

Don't spend your time wishing you *had* something first (a job) and *then* after you will *be* a certain way and *then* you will start to *do* the right things. For example, don't say, "Once I *have* the manager's job, I'll start *doing* my job better and I will *be* responsible." You need to be, do, and then have. This means that you say, "I will *be* more responsible now and therefore *do* a better job and then they will want to promote me and I will be offered/*have* the manager's job." Once you can master this idea (in the correct order) you will be well and truly on your way to success in anything. This concept is also related to giving value first and attracting a great result.

For more information on this technic go to www.scottsbook.com/achieveanything/startnow

KEY POINTS

CHAPTER 13 – ACT AS IF

- From the moment you decide to act as if, the results you will have will be truly astounding.

- You need to be, do, and then have.

- If you see someone getting the results you want, copy them.

Chapter 14. Mini or massive action

You start with a mess before reaching success.

Now you need to execute on the plan you created. You can begin with a mini or massive action to get things moving in your new direction. Mini or massive is not defined and really depends on what your perception is. For some people, getting out of bed 15 minutes earlier every day could be considered a mini action and not that difficult or life-changing. Someone else might consider this a massive action that is a real challenge for them. In addition, this action may be built upon by using that extra 15 minutes to build another habit like writing, investing, learning, or building a side hustle.

It is up to you to decide what magnitude of change you think is good for you and your personal circumstances. Regardless, you need to start doing at least one thing better and repeat it every day. Build this one action into a habit. Then, after a few days or weeks, add another action so you'll have two new habits. As you add more action and habits, you'll see exciting changes in your life and you'll be inspired to continue and do more.

I. The knowing-doing gap

Right! Now we need to start taking action. You can start with baby steps and move on to massive action. Otherwise, we can dive right in the deep end. Either way, one of the biggest hurdles you are likely to face is the knowing-doing gap. Lots of people have read the books or the articles, or listened to a friend or a coach, and heard the information about what they need to do. When it's mentioned that they need to do it, these people say, "I know." And they probably do know. However, many people will then either spend too much time thinking about it, wondering how they will do it, forgetting to do it, or thinking it's just too big and getting almost scared of doing anything. So the critical point here is leaping over the knowing-doing gap.

The need to produce results

This knowing-doing gap should be a very insignificant matter, though it can expand into a very huge problem if left unchecked. In order to be successful, you need to produce results. So, you need to switch your thinking from a consumption mindset (input focus — such as reading books, listening to podcasts, watching videos, or even eating) to a production mindset (output focus — like writing a book, producing a podcast or video, or exercising). So rather than having an input focus where you absorb things, you need to produce results!

This is where a lot of people get thrown off track. They will think about the topic, procrastinate, or avoid the situation entirely, because they're uncertain about how to do it and they don't yet have the confidence to simply blast through by taking action in any way to get going. People get stuck in the middle of this thought process gap. Unfortunately, they can then languish there for days, months and even years.

How do you know if you, or someone else, is stuck in this knowing-doing gap? Listen to what they say and watch what they do. Typically they will say the words, "I know." They will say this when someone tries to point out what they need to do or should be doing to get the results they claim they would like. It will be repeated if someone gives them instructions or advice or tries to remind them of what they've learned and what they need to do to achieve the result they crave. This is a very difficult place to be, as the person believes there is no real problem because they know the right thing to do. You can remain in this deceptive loop for a very long time and not achieve anything.

There is another personality trait that can be highlighted here. The need to know more. This can be seen in the perpetual student. This trait is noticeable if they have done 6 similar courses on the same subject. Or perhaps they are in need of a doctorate before they get moving. Sometimes when this trait is present, it can be because the person does not want to make any errors. With this is mind, they spend more time learning, studying and reading until they feel confident enough to take action. This is often called analysis-paralysis. In the context of the knowing-doing gap, the person is trying to close the gap by focusing on the knowing rather than the doing. Be clear on what you need to learn and do that only. Then get back to action.

The challenging part is not to just nod and think "Yes! I know what to do now. I'll be fine. I'll get there. It will all work out." It might work out, but it is usually dependent on you doing things and taking steps toward achieving the end goal. Just by knowing what needs to be done (Awareness) you will not achieve a result (Production).

When you want to know who is a player and who is a spectator regarding the matter to hand, keep the following quote in mind.

> "As I grow older, I pay less attention to what men say. I just watch what they do."
>
> **–Andrew Carnegie**

II. Procrastination

Watch what people do. They will either be getting the next thing done on their list, toward their goal, or they'll be doing anything but the thing they are supposed to be doing. I'm sure most of us have had those moments when some work or taxes weren't getting done but the house and garage were looking tidy. We can all find that stuff we've been putting off when there is something we find even more challenging on our plate. We will clean the house, tidy papers, declutter a room or the garage, have a snack, turn the tv on, have a nap, etc.

You will also be able to self-diagnose and become aware of your own knowing-doing gap. You will realize when there are things you know you should be doing but are avoiding.

"Only put off until tomorrow what you are willing to die having left undone."

–Pablo Picasso

Starting by doing something on the path you need to follow is a good step. It is critical to move you closer to success.

Law of Diminishing Intent (LDI)

This is a critical point in any goal-achievement process. If you are going to achieve a goal, you will be required to take action to produce a result. It is at this point, when you know something needs to be done, that you need to take immediate action and produce a result. Any action. If you do not take immediate action, you will begin to suffer the consequences of the Law of Diminishing Intent (LDI). This law states "The longer you wait to do something you should do now, the greater the odds that you will never actually do it." It is critical that you get your head around this point. So, let's repeat it and think it through. "The longer you wait to do something you should do now, the greater the odds that you will never actually do it."

You will have recognized this in your life. You may not have known what to call it, but almost certainly you will have experienced the feeling before. For example, your friend's birthday is coming up in two weeks. You have known this happens on the same day now for many years. And two weeks away, you think you have plenty of time to find a good card, purchase it, write something nice inside, get to the post office, and post it off so she receives it several days early. Then you think that you will sort it out tomorrow on your lunch break. Then tomorrow arrives and work is hectic so you can't do it and you decide you will do it on another day. Slowly the days pass and other priorities arise. With each passing day, this task of getting the card and sending it seems to be less possible. It seems to be slipping away from you. Then you realize the birthday is tomorrow and you can't get the card to her in time. So you say you will do it next year and be better prepared. This is how most of these situations end. However, sometimes the LDI continues on for years as there is no deadline, but the desire to take action is almost invisible so it never makes it back on the priority list. Sometimes, you just need to acknowledge that it will never get done and let it go from your life.

> *"The difference between 'must' and 'should' is the life you want and the life you have."*
>
> **–Tony Robbins**

So it is at this point that you need to take some sort of action. This first step is critical. As Zig Ziglar would say, "I've never met anyone who did the second step, if they didn't take the first step first." Immediately upon thinking about the result you want, you must take some sort of action to move toward that result. This action can be small, or small and numerous, all the way up to some massive action. But you need to do something immediately. The small action could be as simple as booking one or two dates and times in your diary now to make a phone call, do an internet search, reflect on your goal or brainstorm. By starting with this initial action, you will greatly increase your chances of success. This is especially true if your initial action is to put a series of date and time slots into your diary to work on this project. Do this using The 7-Day Success Cycle which we outlined earlier.

III. Prepare to struggle before success

Success rarely happens overnight. If you have ever tried to be successful, in a positive way, you know it can take some time. Not only that, but you will also need patience because your early efforts are rarely your best. It usually takes a lot of effort and training to be in the top 10% of anything. Prior to that, and certainly at the beginning of any new endeavor, we all need to go through what I call The Mess.

You see, you need to go through the mess before reaching success. That means trying and failing, feeling silly, looking like an amateur, and being uncomfortable. You will need to go through this phase just as anyone else does. It is the first step on your path to success. It is the step we all must take which tests our resolve to achieve what we dreamed of and have committed to. If you will persevere until you make it through this phase, your chances of ultimate success increase dramatically. You need to get through the challenging start before you can get better and then excel. This is how you begin the process of shifting from uncomfortable to unstoppable.

The great news is that once you get moving in the direction of your dreams, things will soon get better. The excitement of movement, in the direction in which you are so keen on, should help you take the rest of those initial little steps.

Bridge the gap, thwart the LDI and head for success!

By taking this simple action of either diarizing, planning, or doing anything else you can do immediately, you have leapt over a very small knowing-doing gap. You've bridged your knowing into the doing and have thwarted the Law of Diminishing Intent (LDI). You are now successfully on the path to achieving the result you set out to achieve. Well done! All it takes is a little action.

> *"Successful people do what unsuccessful people are not willing to do. Don't wish it were easier; wish you were better."*
>
> **–Jim Rohn**

Your turn

When you take the reins, you get the gains.

So why don't you set your phone timer or watch for five minutes, right now. You can use the five-minute countdown timer. Go ahead and diarize dates for your big goal now. Put a few dates and times in your diary for the next week. Do two or three weeks if you can see that far out. Sometimes it is as simple as turning some of your weekly actions into recurring actions. If you are feeling ambitious, use The 7-Day Success Cycle, which we covered earlier, to book time every day for the weeks ahead.

Set aside time for when you are going to be committed to, and focused on, production of these results you are looking for. I'll see you back here in five minutes so we can complete this action chapter and start achieving the results you want. Drop a bookmark in here or bend the corner of the page to easily find this spot after you are done. Go ahead and diarize dates and times for your big goal now.

Tick-tock

Tick-tock

Tick-tock

Okay. I bet you're feeling great now! You've taken that first step. You are already on the way to achieving the goal you wanted. Congratulations!

Once you've taken the first of maybe 1,000 steps, it's much easier to take the second, third and fourth step. With each step, you will gain that important momentum, that feeling of control, and the confidence in your ability to produce and thrive. You just need to follow the path and go a little farther each time. You will continue to get closer to the result you want until finally you arrive at your destination.

Remember, if you have taken this action above and diarized some dates and times over the next week, then you are one of the few who will consistently achieve your goals. However, if you did not take five minutes and diarize the next week's dates and times, (of when you would set aside time to specifically work on the results you're trying to achieve), then go and do it! Do it right now!

If you did do the activity earlier, then you can take a moment to feel pleased in the fact that you are the one in 100 people on the planet to take that kind of initial initiative.

Ninety-nine percent of people don't take effective action to change their lives. Do you want to be in the 1% of people who do?

Tick-tock

Tick-tock

Tick-tock

It's so easy to do, you might think you'll do it later. But it's so easy not to do right now too. This may create a habit of procrastination and you may not do it later either. Then the Law of Diminishing Intent will grab hold of your goal and drag it into Neverland. So go do it right now!

Alright then, having done that first exercise, you can confirm, to yourself and everyone else, that you are a producer, an action taker. And producers generate results like the one you're trying to achieve. So you have moved from being a consumer to a producer or creator. You've shifted from being the kind of person who nods and says, "I know" to one of the few people who say, "I do" or "I did." You can now say, "I do, I have done, I am doing and will continue to do!" Now that you are a producer, you are a step closer to being an achiever and realizing your goal!

KEY POINTS

CHAPTER 14 – MINI OR MASSIVE ACTION

- › The knowing-doing gap must be quickly recognized and bridged.

- › Now you need to produce results. You need to switch your thinking from a consumption mindset to a production mindset

- › Watch what people do. It will tell you a lot about what you need to know.

‣ Law of Diminishing Intent (LDI). This law states "The longer you wait to do something you should do now, the greater the odds that you will never actually do it."

‣ Get through the mess before success.

‣ Shift from consumer to producer, or creator, in both mindset and your actions.

STEP 5

ACTIONS... TO HELP YOU *ACT*

‣ Take action now. Everything begins in the mind, but decisive action is then needed - it's not just in the thinking of things that makes them happen. It is in the effort of doing.

‣ Let your mind be open to possibilities. The right mindset is required

‣ Decide what magnitude of change you think is good for you and your personal circumstances.

‣ Start doing at least one thing better and repeat it every day. Build this one action into a habit.

‣ Leap over the knowing-doing gap.

‣ Take the first step today. You know what it is.

‣ Take a simple action such as diarizing immediately to leap over a very small knowing-doing gap.

STEP 6 - **REVIEW**

Now you are moving into unstoppable mode. You've done a great job of thinking about a better life, overcoming obstacles, writing out your dreams, preparing a plan, and taking action to move yourself forward. Congratulations! So far, so good. Reading this book is a step on your way to achieving anything. You have either learned some things or remembered things you already knew. And this time you have taken some additional actions based on the tips and tricks you've found here and possibly elsewhere.

All the activity up until now has helped you to shift from being uncomfortable with something. You have a stronger mind and rock solid resolve. You know how to deal with setbacks and continue moving forward on your mission. You are becoming more comfortable with your daily actions and can start to see and feel the power of cause and effect.

If you have been making some of the changes I have outlined in the book, you will already be aware of some aspects of your life being a little different. You may be feeling more confident, more in control, and a little bit happier that you are succeeding. It might remind you of how you felt after getting your stabilizers off your bike as a kid. Or maybe how it felt when you were mastering some tricky math concepts or a skill in music or a sport. It is a wonderful, smile-inducing feeling that you are getting it, that you have begun and you're moving forward.

Now we need to keep going. Keep that growing feeling alive. Most importantly, don't slide back into old habits from here. One of the key ways to do this is to take note of your daily activities and the progress you are making. By tracking your results and taking a little time to review how things are going, you reinforce your success and note areas you may need to celebrate or adjust.

Chapter 15. Achieve & believe

The wonderful thing about progressing things is that you build a data set. This can really help you notice how you are improving and where work remains. And for all the people who prefer the saying, "I'll believe it when I see it," this is your moment to see it and become a believer.

I. Achieve smaller goals

Most people will start with a few smaller goals. These are critical building blocks to success. It might be simple things like getting your feet on the floor when your alarm goes off rather than hitting snooze. Or making your bed every day, as soon as you are up, for the next seven days. Some of you will begin walking an extra 5-10 minutes per day.

The hardest part

It doesn't matter too much what these smaller goals are. It is more important that you make them so easy that you are successful with them. This really could be the hardest part. Removing old habits and adding new ones is often far harder than improving on a habit you already have. These first steps of adjustment are the truly hard part. They may make you feel as uncomfortable as crossing your arms the opposite way or writing with your other hand. However, with time and effort, you will get more comfortable day by day.

Track

Remember to keep track of your activity and results. There are different ways to do this. At various times I've tried several of these that I note below. This tracking system is a very critical habit to develop. I know this makes it slightly more challenging in that you are trying to develop one new habit and I am asking you to double that to two! However, this tracking concept is good for life. And you will be fairly familiar with it if you have ever been to school where they give you grades, or learned an instrument, skill, or sport. You can see if you are improving or not, by how much and over what time frame.

The key here is that, with tracking, you are more likely and more quickly going to be able to shift from this growing comfort position to being unstoppable. This is the magic trick that shifts people from amateur to professional and from professional to legend. An amateur may "go to the gym," or "work out." However, a professional can tell you how often they go, what exercises they do, the number of reps and sets, days on and days off, and where they were and where they are heading.

Legends like basketball stars Michael Jordan and Kobe Bryant knew how many made shots they needed to sink at every training session. It certainly wasn't one or two or some number based on the training concept of, "I will see how I feel." For example, Kobe had a target of 800 made jump shots during practice.

You don't have to aim for legendary status, but you are well-advised to use tips, tactics, and technics that the best have used in order to build your best life ever. Reduce the friction you may encounter on your road to success. Set up your environment to support your goals. Be precise and don't leave it to chance. This will take extra effort, but your results will come quicker and last longer if you do this.

Tips for tracking:

- Buy a separate notepad or journal to record your progress. Be consistent and write in it every day. Get the headlines down like date, time, activity, and results.

- **Buy a calendar.** Every time you do the thing you say you want to adjust, mark a big green checkmark across the box of that date. Then you will start to see your winning streak unfolding. You will not want to break the streak, so it will help you stay on track.
- **Use your Notes section in your phone.** You can add more text when you want. It is always with you, so it is easy to add additional information or analyze your progress when you have a few minutes in a queue.

Appreciate all progress

Notice your achievements, no matter how small you think they are. Like atoms, they may be small but they are the building blocks of everything we know. Your habits are like the atoms and they are the building blocks of your life. With better habits, you will have better results. Those better results will make your life even more exciting and you will feel unstoppable. With some of these basic habits in place, repeated daily, you will find yourself quite able to shift and adjust anything much more easily and quickly.

Celebrate daily how you are controlling your thoughts and actions to bring you closer to the ultimate results you seek. Creating a positive-emotion link with your success will drive your mind to repeat the process to get the positive emotion again.

II. Getting movement

This is a good time to remember Sir Isaac Newton's first law of motion. If a body is at rest, it remains at rest until an external force acts upon it. Consider this book the external force and your actions the requisite movement required to get things going.

Now that you are moving forward with your actions and getting some positive results, you will want to build that momentum. Moving from inaction to action in a certain direction is difficult, but once you start, you need to keep going and maybe even pick up a bit of speed. This is similar to riding a bike. You need to get it moving and then a little more to keep it from falling over and having to start again. It takes more mind and body energy to restart than it does to simply keep it moving a little and staying on it. Same thing applies to habits. Get some momentum going. Some days it will feel a bit uphill and other days it will feel easy with the wind behind you and moving down a slight hill. Enjoy the easier days and be resolute on the tougher days. It is the tougher days that build your resolve and prove you can do this.

III. Growing confidence

As with riding a bike, playing an instrument, or performing school work, your confidence will build based on your results. But it is not just your results. The frequency of your results will make a big difference, as will your consistency. Achieving small goals or milestones will also be more beneficial than simply working toward only one goal several years from now. People like to feel they are making progress. There is a great feeling associated with achievement. It is a strong emotion and keeps humans continually trying to achieve goals.

Each time you achieve your objective, you should celebrate and make it a moment with a strong emotion. Do a fist pump, shout, say your mantra in a strong voice, strike a winner's pose, be fully engaged in the delight of the moment. You see tennis players do this many times in a match. They are continually celebrating for each play or point they did well with. They do not wait until the very end of the match. Keeping yourself strong and supported helps to keep you going during the moments you are not doing so well.

Celebrating is something to do for fun and to build confidence. It gives us a way to feel good about ourselves and our accomplishments. When we celebrate, we are reinforcing something important to us. By making it a more emotion-driven act, you are embedding the feelings of success, winning, and achievement into your psyche. Since we make decisions based on emotion, and then search for supporting evidence to support those decisions, linking strong positive emotional reactions to our wins will encourage us to repeat that habit loop.

As you celebrate your small successes, and they become more numerous, you will begin to develop a winning mindset. Your confidence will grow and you will begin entering states of flow. That is to say that you will start doing your daily habits without thinking, as they become part of you and your life. In taking these actions, you will be building the flywheel of unstoppability. You will have more energy and ability to stay the course while maintaining or even increasing momentum. You will increase your success mass and begin to attract, like gravity, other successful people and opportunities. Just as larger celestial bodies exert a stronger gravitational pull, so do more successful people. People tend to want to be a part of that success orbit, so to speak.

When you hear the phrase, "the rich get richer and the poor get poorer," it does have a link to finance and wealth, but also health, fitness, relationships, knowledge, and enjoyment. At its heart, and underlying this phrase, is a mindset. You either build an abundance mindset or a scarcity mindset. Depending on which you build, you will attract more of that into your life. I suggest reading this paragraph again. As I wrote in chapter 2, mindset is absolutely critical for success. (Note: the quote is quite general. It should say that people with the right mindset get richer and those who don't have a good mindset get poorer. But it doesn't roll off the tongue as easily nor does it feed people's negative money bias as much.)

Increase the belief in yourself and benefit more from the cause-and-effect system of the universe. Continue to do this as you see action, momentum, and early results. You are shifting into unstoppable. You've got this.

KEY POINTS

CHAPTER 15 – ACHIEVE & BELIEVE

> A few smaller goals are critical building blocks to success.

> The start is the hardest part. Know that and get going. It gets easier.

> Be resolute on the tougher days – they are the ones that build character and confidence.

> As you celebrate your small successes, and they become more numerous, you will begin to develop a winning mindset. Your confidence will grow and you will begin entering states of flow. That is to say that you will start doing your daily habits without thinking, as they become part of you and your life.

> As you achieve more, you will attract others into your success orbit.

Chapter 16. Course-correct

Have you ever noticed that the only time you need to correct something is when you are off course or wrong? You don't need to do anything when things are on course or you are correct.

Let's use your experience riding a bicycle or driving a car. You are continuously making super small adjustments to your steering to keep yourself on course. If you let yourself drift, you might end up quite some ways away from where you had intended to go.

One of the great benefits of writing things down while tracking is that you can use that data to help you course-correct. If you were supposed to exercise four times over the past week and you've only done three days by Friday, you will know you have to get out there and exercise tomorrow. It is important to write the data down because it is easy enough to confuse the days and weeks that have passed with others. You may think you went on a certain day when you were actually thinking of the previous week. Tracking your activity by writing it down will ensure that you are able to keep on track and be accountable. Yes, it is a little extra work. However, you will greatly increase your probability of success. Your self-esteem will rise as well as you keep your promises and commitments to yourself.

I. Airplanes: From manual to autopilot

An airplane can be flown manually or on autopilot. It has been common since planes were invented that they take off and land in manual mode. That remains the case, though many pilots engage the autopilot once safely at cruising altitude. This may change as we enter the driverless era. Perhaps planes will be flown without human pilots. That would be interesting to get your head around.

Until that time, we can still use the airplane as the example. The pilot is like the mind while the cockpit controls are the brain and the aircraft is like our body. The pilot decides what to do, gives the signals for that to happen via the controls, and then the plane responds to those control commands. As with the evolution of the airplane, when you are creating a new habit, you should maintain specific attention and complete control. Being deliberate in your actions, and doing them yourself, ensures that they will get done reasonably well. Though once we do a specific activity the same way, numerous times, it gets encoded in our mind and we soon learn to do that thing without deliberate thinking.

That is what autopilot is to an airplane. A serious of actions to be undertaken under a set of specific circumstances. As soon as it is clear and consistent, it can be automated and that is the same for your habits. Once a habit becomes so rule-based and habitual, your mind can set it to automatic and you will not have to think much about it. Ultimately, it becomes part of your flow. When you hit a flow state, that is when you try to stop and analyze your activity, and that is when the problems occur.

Adjusting

The great thing about tracking and reviewing is that they allow you to quickly notice when something is going a little off course. Then, the adjustment required to get back on course is minimal, with limited loss of time or effort. The longer you leave things veering off course, the greater the challenge of getting back on course and the greater the likelihood of other unintended consequences.

For example, imagine a plane flying from London, England to São Paulo, Brazil. While flying south over the Atlantic Ocean, the flight continued to veer slightly east. Even just a degree at a time. Over such a long distance, without tracking or reviewing its flight path, the plane could find itself beyond São Paulo and somewhere over the south Atlantic between Tierra del Fuego, Argentina and Cape Town, South Africa. Not only would they be well off course but they would have flown hours beyond their destination and used much more fuel than they had planned to or had on board. In addition, they would still be hours away from any ground where they could land the plane and probably be running out of jet fuel. These are pretty dire unintended consequences. However, I use this to highlight the critical importance of frequently tracking and reviewing details and course-correcting promptly.

Learning from others

With nearly 8 billion people alive on the planet today and more than 100 billion humans having ever lived on this spinning rock, someone almost certainly will have done what you want to do. Knowing that, and having internet search ability and books, you should be able to see how others have done something before you. Whether you want to sail across the ocean, shed 15 pounds, quit smoking or increase your income and wealth, there will be a template, or many, that you could follow. What they used to track their progress will be published somewhere and you can simply follow their lead. This might help you save time and effort by having you track the more relevant items and metrics, which make the greatest impact. This is one way to plan and course-correct quicker than doing it all on your own.

Keep distractions at bay

A useful way to keep course-corrections at a minimum is to keep distractions at bay. If you are keeping focused on the outcome you want, and being relentless in your actions to get there, you are more likely to achieve anything you want.

Being focused is one side of the coin. You need to match this with not getting distracted, or at least keeping distractions to a minimum. So, while you are pushing forward with focus, guard the back door against distractions.

Distractions will slow you down, shift you off course, and even reduce your belief and confidence. One distraction is fine if it is for a short time. However, you must guard against the time lost, the mental fatigue it contributes to, the follow-on distractions it creates, and letting distractions become a habit in your life.

Accountability

There are several ways to develop better habits with focus and without distractions. One way to focus is to insert some accountability into the process. If you have someone who you must report in to, you are more likely to stay focused and get the job done. You can see how this works in many settings. Some examples would be getting a report in to a teacher, completing a project for your boss at work, and having a fitness friend you work out with. You do not want to let them down nor do you want to let yourself down or diminish your good brand with them.

In addition, you can strengthen your focus if you create accountability by having a mindset mate or use a countdown timer. The mindset mate will encourage you to stay focused and may talk you through any distraction or lack of focus. They will also applaud you and cheer you on when you do succeed in remaining focused and completing goals. The countdown timer is useful if you set it for short bursts. If you set it for 15 minutes, you can see how much you can accomplish in that time period. When the timer goes off, you can reset it again and keep pushing, or set it for 5 minutes to take a break. This helps to ensure you don't turn a five-minute break into an afternoon off. Every time the timer goes off, you reset it for your next sprint of activity. For those of you who like to have an official method to reference, you can look up Pomodoro Technique, which is similar.

If you work better with an emotional push to force you over the line and get things done, here is another angle I sometimes use. Imagine you are a Marine and your life is on the line, behind enemy lines. Your effort and success are life-and-death matters for you and your team. You must work quickly, intelligently, and without pause. No time for a tv binge or raid on the fridge. It is a matter of get it done and do it well or pain and death await you.

Some things need to be taken seriously in life. Are you giving your goals and dreams the right level of attention, effort, and commitment?

Deadline

Finally, having a firm deadline with consequences can be excellent to help you focus and remain undistracted. Time pressure is a great way to get focused and complete things. You see this all the time in movies when someone has to race against time to diffuse a bomb or stop the baddie. The tv show 24 is springing to mind at the moment. Although you will also be familiar with the "deadline means focus" concept if you have ever had a school assignment, work commitment, plane to catch, or birthday to organize.

Remember, your whole life could drift right by if you do not focus on short- and long-term outcomes, with deadlines and consequences that matter to you. Then you need to continually check in with your progress toward those goals. If your goals remain relevant and you are able to keep course-correcting with small adjustments, then carry on.

However, sometimes our previously set goals are no longer in line with our new view of our future. Or, we may have gotten so off course that small adjustments are no longer practical or useful in getting us back on track. When these more significant situations arise, it can be better to make a conscious decision to pivot.

II. Pivot point
(if getting off course gets out of hand)

We often know when a useful pivot point is reached. Sometimes we don't like to admit it or acknowledge it, but it is a good idea to reflect on it for a few minutes.

A good safety net to have is a pivot point of your choosing, sometime in the future, when you set out to achieve something. This pivot point can be personal to you and may be time-based, event-driven, or based on your feelings, such as pleasure or pain.

To illustrate this more easily, let's look at a few samples. If your goal was to complete a four-year degree (time-based), you would be able to check out how you were doing at the end of each semester and see if you were on track. If you failed a course, you would have to do a night class or a summer course to catch up. Otherwise, you would need to allow 4.5 years so you could complete the last course at the end of your expected four-year period.

It's never too early to pick a desired retirement date either. Then you can work back from that date and figure out what you need to do to make it a reality. The earlier you can set the desired date, the more time you will have to make it a reality in your life. The feeling of pleasure from being able to retire may be quite strong (feelings). Although you are best to have a few plans of other things to do after that date. Retirement is, ideally, a pivot point where you no longer exchange time for money, but rather time for additional enjoyment. For many people, this will start around 65-70 years of age. However, in exceptional circumstances you could retire at 25.

With good planning and following the outlines in this book, you may be able to retire comfortably at 38, 42 or 57. Some people will never retire in the traditional sense because what they did all their life for money is what brought them their greatest enjoyment. So even in their advancing years, they might continue to occupy themselves with their profitable pastime. You see this in people like Warren Buffet, Alice Cooper, and Clint Eastwood.

Finally, if starting a business, you may choose a specific situation to mark as your pivot point (event-driven). This point may come if you have spent the $50,000 of start-up investment you allocated. Or it could be when you reach a certain number of customers or amount of revenue. The pivot may be the extreme reaction, such as shutting the company down, or a more modest change in direction.

I recall TripAdvisor founder Stephen Kaufer noting how the company had to pivot a couple of times from their original model. The company started in 2000, but only with reviews from established sources. By early 2001, they explored and trialled the idea of letting customers put up their own reviews. Soon, that was the only type of review on the site. In addition, they had to revisit their original idea of selling ads on the site. By the end of 2001, the company had a new, dominant income stream based on a small referral fee from each company that a site visitor clicked on.

So whether you are aiming to achieve a fitness, financial, company, career, or lifestyle goal, you are well-advised to set out some pivot point moments in advance. By knowing where and when you may need to pivot, you may prepare yourself better with tracking and course-correcting so a pivot may never be needed.

KEY POINTS

CHAPTER 16 – COURSE-CORRECT

› Track and adjust to stay on course. Your self-esteem will rise as you keep your promises and commitments to yourself.

› Once a habit becomes so rule-based and habitual, your mind can set it to automatic and you will hardly have to think about it.

› The great thing about tracking and reviewing is that they allow you to quickly notice when something is going a little off course.

› While you are pushing forward with focus, guard the back door against distractions.

› One way to focus is to insert some accountability into the process.

› Are you giving your goals and dreams the right level of attention, effort and commitment?

› A firm deadline with consequences can be excellent to help you focus and remain undistracted.

› Prepare a pivot point. But with good tracking and course-correcting, you may never need it.

Chapter 17. Repeat

This may be the easiest part in the Review Step, but it still requires that you do it! Hopefully, you are tracking well and reviewing frequently and course-correcting as you go.

Repetition is how we learn. It is also how we excel and scale a process or business. The challenge is that repeating something accurately and frequently can get a little bit boring. This is true even if you love the thing you are repeating. The repetition boredom conundrum is one we all face. It is possibly why only a few people can make it to excellence in any given field. It is what it takes to become unstoppable. So at the start, learn to love the reps. Each accurate repetition will bring you closer to the result you are looking for.

Once you have a process well in hand, you should write it down, systematize it, gamify it, review, and smile. Then, often-repeated and systemic activities can be delegated. Fascinating.

Just like our earlier example of an airplane on autopilot, you are going to bundle together this series of habits you have developed through tracking and course-correcting. This bundle of habits can be systematized and elevated as a whole system rather than as individual components. Similar to autopilot, there will be a variety of metrics that you will now be repeatedly tracking and adjusting for throughout your life.

I. Written log

The first step is to write out your metrics. Note down what you are tracking, when, how you course-correct and how you review those corrections. You may already have this written down, from earlier, which would be great. However, if you do not, then please take a few minutes now and write out some headlines or bullet points to get you started.

If you don't write these points down, you are unlikely to remember all the points, all of the time. This will make your efforts less effective and may reduce the speed and magnitude of your success.

Ideally you will keep this information in one place, such as a journal, as we have covered earlier in the book. A journal is great because it keeps things in one place and is therefore easy to look back through to spot trends, progress, and your success. It is also easy to take with you to work or on holiday so you can keep pressing forward with your goals wherever you are.

II. Gamify your progress

Now one of the best ways to help make your endeavors more successful is to make the process fun or even gamify it. In addition to stating, "I am (insert desired mindset or state — like happy, grateful, determined, slim, effective, or well spoken)" making things fun is another surefire way to increase the likelihood of your success. When an activity is enjoyable (positive emotional impact), you are more likely to repeat it. Think of all the things you happily do, like go out with friends, watch a movie, play mini golf, or travel. These are things you would happily repeat because you enjoy them. Try to find the joy button for the activities you are interested in making into habits. Sometimes it helps to start with some mental tricks and illusions to get the ball rolling.

Mental tricks and illusions

In order to gamify something, it can be helpful to use some mental tricks and illusions. There are various types you can use and I will note a few of them below.

- **Pretend you are the best person you can think of who has achieved this goal.** As we learned before, you can increase your probability of success by acting as if you are already the best. It is not about being full of yourself. Rather, it is about thinking like that brilliant person and developing their habits.

- **Use the, "I am" phrase to start your sentences.** Ensure that the phrase is followed by the mental or physical state you wish to achieve. If you are trying to meditate, you may repeat to yourself, "I am calm." When trying to shift some weight from 165 pounds to 145 pounds, keep saying to yourself, "I am becoming a 145-pound person and feel great."

- **Get a mantra that makes you smile** and repeat this to yourself several times while you are working on your goals. This is especially important when things are not going your way as much as you would like. To build your money mindset, try repeating, "I am a money magnet." Another option would be, "I have a millionaire mindset."

- **Try to keep a streak going.** Get up at 05:55am for all the days in a row that you can. Yes, even Saturday and Sunday. Your body and mind enjoy consistency.

- **Build on your success.** For example, go out and walk for one minute or 100 meters today. Then make it two minutes or 200 meters tomorrow. In two weeks, you may be up to 14 minutes or 1.4 kilometers.

- **Eat one mouthful less.** When dieting, it can be handy to simply take one spoonful less of each item during the day. Do this every day, at each meal and snack, or as frequently as you can, and soon you will have reduced your calorie intake by a sufficient amount and you will be meeting your fitness goals in no time.

- **Send your success and challenges to a friend in a text.** This has the triple impact of writing it down for review later, reinforcing it in your mind by thinking and writing it, and providing social proof of your attempts and success, acting as an accountability mechanism. You may even get feedback for your efforts and hopefully some cheerleading.

III. Review and smile

Make an appointment with yourself every day to review your activity and progress. Hopefully, you will start to notice some small trends in the direction you are looking for. Perhaps you will be 0.2 of a pound lighter or you are now walking 7 minutes per day or you have woken up at 5 a.m. for six days in a row. If you have some financial goals, maybe you will have reviewed your accounts 6 days in a row or put $1 per day in your new investment account. It will all be exciting, and hopefully you will be feeling positive about starting your new actions, regardless of the immediate results.

Sometimes you will notice it takes a few attempts or many days to start getting the feedback or results that you would be happy with. And success is not always a straight line. Nor do results happen immediately. Sometimes things will go better than expected and at other times they will be worse. There will even be occasions when you work hard at something and the desired result isn't there or things even go backward. Yikes!!! Be calm and carry on, as that is all part of the ups and downs in life. The key parts are to become aware, course-correct, and carry on. This is the transition stage when you are shifting through the uncomfortable reality of today, starting where you are and doing something new. It is work. It can be uncomfortable both physically and especially mentally. But push through!

The discomfort is proof that you are working on the new you. As you continue to normalize this discomfort and adapt to the adjustment in your life, you will notice the shift you've made. Continue along on this path and as discomfort gives way to resilience, determination and confidence, you will continue to shift into the unstoppable zone.

Smile

Every day, when you are reviewing what you have done, remember to smile. The simple idea that you are sitting down to review anything means you are making progress! You may not see these steps and structural activities as success or progress, but that's what they are. These are the foundations and building blocks of success that you must have before the outcomes and results you are seeking can become a reality. Examples of these are having developed an awareness of the review tactic, having consciously set a goal you are striving for, and having taken some action that could be tracked or reviewed.

Remember, these are all ingredients to success that you were either not aware of or not doing consistently before. For this reason alone you should be smiling. You should be grinning from ear to ear as you read this right now. Finding, reading, and thinking about the ideas in this book are all major contributors to your future success. Every step along the route to your final destination helps shift you along the continuum from uncomfortable to unstoppable. Yes, it will take some time and there will be bumps in the road and obstacles that appear in your way. However, you are building the foundations for all future success with these structures. So be sure to smile as you review your previous day. You are building the mental muscles that deliver results in the not-too-distant future.

Smile that you started! Smile that you have continued! Smile at your discipline! Smile at your results! (All of them! Big and small.)

KEY POINTS

CHAPTER 17 – REPEAT

> ‣ Repetition is how we learn. It is also how we excel and scale a process or business.

> ‣ Systematize repeated activities so they are easy to do or can be delegated.

> ‣ Success is not always a straight line. Nor do results happen immediately. The key parts are to become aware, course-correct, and carry on.

> ‣ Press on and continue to shift through the discomfort and into the unstoppable zone!

> ‣ Remember, these are all ingredients to success that you were either not aware of, repeating or not doing consistently before. Now that you know, go do it and close the gaps (both the knowing-doing gap and the expectation v reality gap).

STEP 6

ACTIONS... TO HELP YOU *REVIEW*

> ‣ Keep track of your activity and results.

> ‣ Use the Tips for tracking section in Chapter 15.

> ‣ Celebrate daily how you are controlling your thoughts and actions to bring you closer to the ultimate results you seek.

> ‣ Review and celebrate because they reinforce good habits.

> ‣ Find and use an accountability partner to keep you on your timeline.

﹥ Note in a journal the variety of metrics that you will now be repeatedly tracking and adjusting for throughout your life.

﹥ Try to find the joy button for the activities you are interested in making into habits.

﹥ Gamify your progress with mental tricks and illusions (see several in Chapter 17).

﹥ Make an appointment with yourself, in your diary, every day to review your activity and progress.

﹥ Smile that you started! Smile that you have continued! Smile at your discipline!

STEP 7 - **CELEBRATE**

Most people look forward to this step and will enjoy this part of the process. Celebrations help tie your success to joyous emotion that should encourage you to do the process again. So I suggest that you develop a frequent celebration style so that you can harness this powerful feedback tool. Think of how tennis players react after a successful shot. Often you will see a clenched fist being snapped toward their chest, their head angles down, and usually a "yes!" or other positive word is formed on their lips. This is often the same for soccer players, golfers, hockey players, and all other sporting people. Others will do this upon receiving exam results, a bonus, or a raise.

It is something we do naturally, especially at very important moments. Now find more moments to adopt this action, or some other emotionally connecting response. The more you create positive feedback loops throughout your day, the more likely you will be to perform the actions required to get them. This is a key ingredient to progressing to and through the unstoppable zone.

There are two challenges, however. The first challenge is to fall in love with the process, not the celebration itself. It is all about the steps that get you to the final event or outcome that should be appreciated and celebrated, not simply the final event or outcome itself. Those who only enjoy the celebrating soon find their bank account has dwindled, their success has vanished, and their reason for celebrating gone. The second challenge is celebrating often enough but not dis-proportionately. You should probably celebrate more often. Especially small but critical celebrations after milestones and daily wins. However, guard against the celebrating becoming more important than the process, activities, and achievements themselves.

Chapter 18. Every little and big goal achievement

The achievement of any goal, no matter what the size, needs to be celebrated. Celebrating milestones is also a good habit to develop. When you take action, celebrate having done it. Don't wait for the result. Celebrate your action regardless of the result. If the result is negative, celebrate learning something – you've obviously just graduated to the next level! Of course, if there is a positive result, celebrate that too! Celebrate the process and the steps not just the outcome.

- Celebrate the weekly savings goals, not just the financial freedom.
- Celebrate having studied, not just the test results.
- Celebrate the early-morning training runs, not just your race result.
- Celebrate saying no to a piece of cake, not just when you lose two pounds.

If we want the results to continue, we must celebrate the action in the process that leads to the result. That way, we are more likely to repeat the action and the cause-and-effect loop will kick in and deliver our intended result, more and more often.

I. Little and often

The key to success is often found in the little things that we do on a daily basis and not one giant action. Tiger Woods did not wake up one day in his late teens and decide he would try to be good at golfing and win the Open the next day. There is a lot of effort that goes into the making of the success we see. We do not get to see the hours of training, studying, rehab, failure, disappointment, and all the restarts. However, without those daily efforts and improvements, the result would not be on display. Think of planting seeds in your garden and how much goes on under the surface before you start to see the potential for results above ground. Anyone who has seen bamboo grow knows this very well too.

Celebrate frequently

Every day you will have an opportunity to celebrate your dedication to the process. Each day you wake up, you have the opportunity to add to your skill and experience by doing a bit more. Teachers at school request that children make weekly progress by following the mantra of "little and often." It is a great phrase and I suggest you adopt it for your own efforts. Another good phrase to remember is the slogan of the UK grocery chain, Tesco, "Every little helps."

These phrases are true for your daily efforts and your daily celebrations. Constantly reinforce good vibes within yourself when you take the actions that will lead to the results you want. This can be simple, like a fist pump, a smile, a positive thought, some nodding, or a bit of clapping. It can also be more involved such as watching a short comedy clip on YouTube, ordering a takeaway, or a quick call with a friend who'll be happy for you.

Proportionality

It is probably a good idea to keep celebrations proportional. This gauge will be yours to choose as you will know the action and the significance of each moment. A great pass in sports, or an attempt on goal, is celebrated differently than scoring a game-winning goal. One is more of a high five moment, while the other may involve a lot of jumping, shouting, and hugging.

It is a good rule of thumb to celebrate the day to day, grinding activities at one level and build up to greater celebrations for key milestones and significant project wins. Naturally, the biggest celebration is usually reserved for the ultimate result. Here you could think of a gold medal win, a shattered world record, collecting your degree, or making the final payment on your car or home.

II. Keep a list of achievements (words, pictures, mementos)

"Out of sight, out of mind," is an important phrase to remember here. There is some truth to this, unless you focus very hard and consistently to keep something at the forefront of your mind. Our mind forgets what isn't frequently in sight. So it is a good idea to keep your achievements in full view. Remember to feel the emotion you had when receiving the result. This will help to tie that success to a good feeling and encourage more success. Remember too, all the effort and grind that went into that result. You worked hard for this result and overcame obstacles that could have sent you off track. Be proud of your determination, efforts, and end result.

A good reason to keep a scrapbook or reward board is that our memories fade with time. We may forget our race time, our score, or our award. The details may shift in our mind with time. You may start to wonder if it was on a Thursday or a Tuesday. Then other details start to slip. These are important elements of success in your life. Treasure these wins because they are the gold of your mind. They are priceless, invaluable and yours.

In your journal, or separate scrapbook of attempts and wins, note down all the good things. It will become a wonderful archive of key moments of your life. It will support you through tougher times. And it is something that can be passed down as a memento for curious children.

Keep powerful memories in sight. Place awards on shelves and hang photos on walls. Look at these often. Comment on them to yourself and remind yourself of their importance in your life. Celebrate their existence. You should keep your journal to hand so that it is easy to book in five minutes a week to flip through it. Keep your wins fresh in mind and your mind will look for opportunities to crave more wins.

III. Plan some nice things

Put some celebration moments in your diary. When you know you will have achieved some success, ensure you have something worthwhile ready to celebrate. Plan a dinner or a party on the day you receive your degree. Book time with friends and family to celebrate the end of a term at school. In your diary, plan celebrations for trying and achieving and not just succeeding with the end goal. Be sure to vary the expense as well. You are best to keep celebrations within your budget. A mix of events that are free, and paid for, is a start. Big celebrations do not have to be elaborate with a big bill attached. Simple things like a phone call, a walk, a picnic, or some "me time" to sit and reflect can be as good or better than a big party, a trip somewhere, or an expensive meal out. Of course different people and moments might call for different celebrations. You can celebrate on your own or with others. There is no right or wrong. Though you really will benefit from doing something.

KEY POINTS

CHAPTER 18 – EVERY LITTLE AND BIG GOAL ACHIEVEMENT

▸ Fall in love with the process.

▸ The steps that get you to the final event or outcome should be appreciated and celebrated.

▸ Celebrate often, especially for each small milestone. But, guard against the celebrating becoming more important than the process, activities, and achievements themselves.

▸ The key to success is often found in the little things that we do on a daily basis and not one giant action.

▸ Keep celebrations proportional.

▸ Keep your achievements in full view. Keep a diary of them too.

Chapter 19. Grow belief and confidence through achievement

Success brings more success. The opposite is also true. An important aspect of celebrating and curating your success is that it helps to build greater confidence and belief in yourself, your abilities, and your determination to take on greater challenges. Two areas that celebrating will impact are pride and determination.

I. Pride

It is good to feel pride. It will help you feel great. Your back will straighten, your posture will improve and you will stretch up to the heavens. It is a lovely feeling to look back on your achievements and know that it was you who did this. It should bring a smile to your face, put a skip in your step, and instill a calmness in your body and soul. Your mind can relax and enjoy the journey all over again.

This sense of pride will also help you build your confidence for your next event. The more you do, the more you'll believe you can do, and this feeling of pride will help support this.

A word of caution here is required. You may know that pride is one of the seven deadly sins and is considered the most serious one by many. Like everything, balance and moderation are important. With pride, be sure to maintain humility to keep it in check. Too much pride can be as detrimental as too little or none.

II. Determination

By celebrating your activities, you will build greater belief in yourself. You will recall the determination required to get you started with something new, to set challenging goals, and to consistently build on your skills. There will be many days that you will not feel like doing what needs to be done. However, you will have shown your resolve and been committed to completing the tasks required. Your determination to see this through will have set you apart, in your own mind, from the old you and possibly from others you may have competed with.

Once again, the feeling of knowing that you directed this movie of your life will greatly increase your level of confidence. Especially as you realize it was your determination that saw you through to the end. It will also encourage and support your belief that you can achieve anything.

KEY POINTS

CHAPTER 19 – GROW BELIEF AND CONFIDENCE THROUGH ACHIEVEMENT

- ‣ Celebrating success helps to build greater confidence and belief in yourself.

- ‣ Two other areas that celebrating will impact are pride and determination.

- ‣ Be proud of your accomplishments.

- ‣ Be determined to complete your commitments, even on days you do not feel like it.

Chapter 20. Gratitude

An excellent way to finish anything is to thank those who have been involved along the way. This is a normal part of life in many areas. We thank people for inviting us somewhere and for making or serving us food. We also thank people who have trained us, educated us, and stopped us from doing something we shouldn't.

The power of gratitude is sometimes overlooked. It is such a simple thing and yet it can make such a difference in the way you move forward. For starters, appreciating or thanking someone is free to do, so there is no financial excuse not to do it. It is also good manners, which is something that is widely taught and admired in those who demonstrate this trait. Additionally, it is a way of giving back to someone as it acknowledges them and their participation in your good fortune. This has the unintended consequence of improving your image, brand, or reputation with that person. The follow-on effects from this good karma can be profound. Unfortunately, it seems to be unmeasurable at the moment, so you will have to rely on belief and anecdotal observations.

One other benefit is that it makes you feel good. The idea that you stop your life to consider someone else and the contribution they have made to your life is wonderful. Then taking it that extra step and actually thanking them and showing your appreciation is definitely a feel-good activity. It's hard not to have this sort of thing bring a smile to your face.

So thank you, dear reader, for taking the time to read this book. I appreciate that you may have spent some money to buy a copy and certainly you have spent time to read through it, if you are reading this part. I hope you have refreshed some old thoughts and picked up some new views and techniques that you can use to more easily make the changes you are looking for in your life.

I appreciate your desire to make positive changes and wish you the very best in all of your endeavors. Hopefully, you have already started using the tips and ideas outlined in this book. If there is more I can help with, or clarify, please let me know. If you have feedback, good or to improve, please get in touch. You can find ways to contact me on social media and at www.scottsbook.com. You will also find other people there like you. We can get through this together and you will continue to shift from uncomfortable to unstoppable on your path to Achieve Anything.

From this point forward, you will be putting in the work. As a person on this planet, I appreciate that. Because this good and positive desire to achieve greater things, or improve yourself and our world, will impact us all in positive ways.

Thank you and best wishes!

KEY POINTS
CHAPTER 20 – GRATITUDE

> ‣ An excellent way to finish anything is to thank those who have been involved along the way.

> ‣ Giving appreciation and a thank you is free, good manners, good karma, and it makes you feel good.

STEP 7

ACTIONS... TO HELP YOU *CELEBRATE*

> - When you take action, celebrate having done it. Celebrate buying this book. Celebrate having read this far. Celebrate your new or renewed awareness of the steps to success.

> - Celebrate your action regardless of the result. If the result is negative, celebrate learning something.

> - Treasure your wins because they are the gold of your mind. They are priceless, invaluable and yours.

> - Place awards on shelves and hang photos on walls.

> - Put some celebration moments in your diary. Book in to celebrate your effort.

> - Celebrate completing this book!

> - Celebrate putting a five-star review of this book on Amazon, Goodreads or your favorite review site. Tag me in and I will celebrate with you!

FINAL WORD

Now it's your turn to have an impact on the world. If you thought this was a useful book for you, then please tell your friends, family, and co-workers to buy or borrow a copy. Let people know on social media, at book club, or your local library. Tell your children. If everyone had this information, understood it, and acted on it, imagine what we, the people of the world, could achieve. As a group, we could achieve anything!

VISIT MY WEBSITE AND SOCIAL MEDIA PAGES

You can follow me, contact me or get involved in the conversations at:

www.scottsbook.com/achieveanything

Instagram is @scottsthinking

Twitter is @scottgregory1

My blog site is at www.scottsthinking.com

LinkedIn account is www.linkedin.com/in/scottgregory1

Clubhouse is @scottsthinking

My Facebook group is Action & Results Thinking

RESOURCES

Visit my blog site at www.scottsthinking.com for a full list of books, videos and other media that have influenced my thinking and can help you further shift yours. A few of the books are:

Rich Dad, Poor Dad by Robert Kiyosaki

The Millionaire Fastlane by MJ DeMarco

You are a Badass by Jen Sincero

Secrets of the Millionaire Mind by T. Harv Eker

Mindset by Carol Dweck

The 7 Habits of Highly Successful People by Stephen Covey

IF YOU FOUND THIS BOOK USEFUL

Please go to amazon.com and leave a review. I would really appreciate it and it helps others discover the book and decide whether it would be a great resource for them.

Other ways to let people know how you feel are:

Goodreads

Instagram

Facebook

LinkedIn

Twitter

Other social media, radio, newspaper, TV, magazines, friends, family and institutions.

If you have feedback you would like to give me in general or for any future update, direct message me on Instagram or send me an email at scott@scottsthinking.com

POSTSCRIPT: NOW, ACHIEVE ANYTHING!

You will achieve *something*. Each day you achieve many things: Staying alive. Waking up each day. Listening. Reading. Breathing. Commuting. Working. Relaxing.

No matter how basic, you will achieve many things every day. So why not make one of those additional achievements something you really want or care about? Write down your big goal or even just your current goal. Tape it to your mirror, bed post or front door. Put it in your underwear drawer, on top of things, and on top of your kitchen counter and dining table. Put it everywhere you will see it several times a day to remind you of it when you veer off track — and you will. You have veered at times, repeatedly, through life so far, so let's assume you will veer a little more still.

Have these notes around to help you course-correct, like an airplane does. When you drift slightly off course, these reminders will help nudge you back on track.

Amazingly, when you start to focus repeatedly on what you actually want and continue to take simple steps toward the end goal on a daily basis, you will achieve anything you set your mind to. Simple to say, a challenge to do, and yet oh so rewarding as you build up a head of steam and complete your goal on your way to becoming unstoppable!

Let's go!

CPSIA information can be obtained
at www.ICGtesting.com
Printed in the USA
LVHW032232230122
709135LV00004B/205